P9-CCL-444

# ENTER THE PHOENIX

A TOM DOHERTY ASSOCIATES BOOK
NEW YORK

This is a work of fiction. All the characters and events portrayed in this book are fictitious, and any resemblance to real people or events is purely coincidental.

MARVEL COMICS' X-MEN #2: ENTER THE PHOENIX!

Originally published in magazine form as X-MEN #100, #101, and as CLASSIC X-MEN #8.



A Tor Book
Published by Tom Doherty Associates, Inc.
175 Fifth Avenue
New York, NY 10010



ISBN: 0-812-54325-4

First printing: January 1996

Printed in the United States of America

0 9 8 7 6 5 4 3 2 1

**Original cover to *X-Men* #101**
artist: Dave Cockrum
art correction: Rob LaQuinta
colorist: Sean Tiffany

**"Greater Love Hath No X-Man"** (*X-Men* #100)
author: Chris Claremont
artist: Dave Cockrum
letterer: Annette Kawecki
editor: Marv Wolfman

**"Like a Phoenix From the Ashes"** (*X-Men* #101)
author: Chris Claremont
penciler: Dave Cockrum
inker: Frank Chiaramonte
letterer: John Costanza
editor: Archie Goodwin

**"The Origin of the Phoenix"** (*Classic X-Men* #8)
author: Chris Claremont
artist: John Bolton
letterer: Tom Orzechowski
editor: Ann Nocenti
editor-in-chief: Jim Shooter

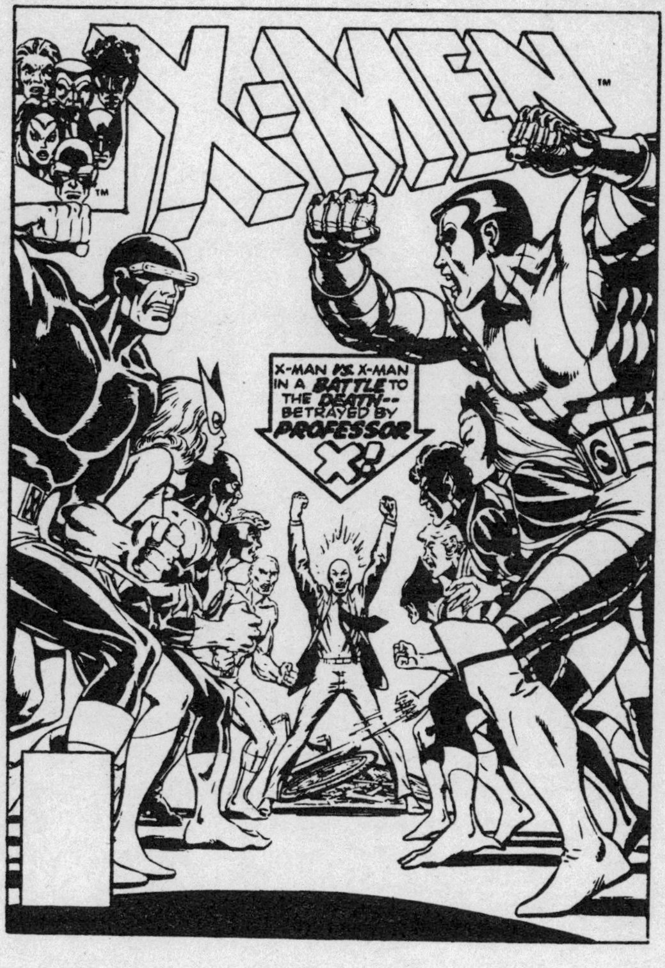
X-MEN™
X-MAN VS. X-MAN IN A BATTLE TO THE DEATH-- BETRAYED BY PROFESSOR X!

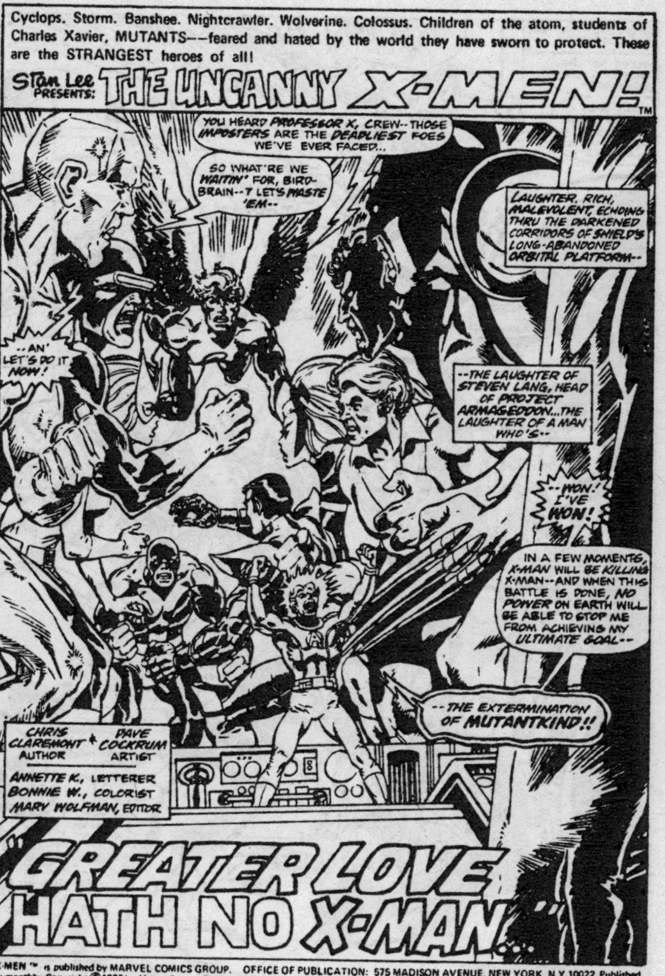

Cyclops. Storm. Banshee. Nightcrawler. Wolverine. Colossus. Children of the atom, students of Charles Xavier, MUTANTS––feared and hated by the world they have sworn to protect. These are the STRANGEST heroes of all!
STAN LEE PRESENTS: THE UNCANNY X-MEN!™
YOU HEARD PROFESSOR X, CREW--THOSE IMPOSTERS ARE THE DEADLIEST FOES WE'VE EVER FACED...
SO WHAT'RE WE WAITIN' FOR, BIRD-BRAIN--? LET'S WASTE 'EM--
--AN' LET'S DO IT NOW!
LAUGHTER, RICH, MALEVOLENT, ECHOING THRU THE DARKENED CORRIDORS OF SHIELD'S LONG-ABANDONED ORBITAL PLATFORM--
--THE LAUGHTER OF STEVEN LANG, HEAD OF PROJECT ARMAGEDDON...THE LAUGHTER OF A MAN WHO'S--
--WON! I'VE WON!
IN A FEW MOMENTS, X-MAN WILL BE KILLING X-MAN--AND WHEN THIS BATTLE IS DONE, NO POWER ON EARTH WILL BE ABLE TO STOP ME FROM ACHIEVING MY ULTIMATE GOAL--
--THE EXTERMINATION OF MUTANTKIND!!
CHRIS CLAREMONT AUTHOR & DAVE COCKRUM ARTIST
ANNETTE K., LETTERER
BONNIE W., COLORIST
MARV WOLFMAN, EDITOR
"GREATER LOVE HATH NO X-MAN..."


X-MEN™ is published by MARVEL COMICS GROUP. OFFICE OF PUBLICATION: 575 MADISON AVENUE, NEW YORK, N.Y.10022. Published bi-monthly. Copyright © 1976 by Marvel Comics Group, A Division of Cadence Industries Corporation. All rights reserved 575 Madison Avenue, N.Y. 10022. Vol. 1, No. 100, August, 1976 issue. Price 25¢ per copy in the U. S. and Canada. Subscription rate $3.50 for 12 issues. Canada $4.25. Foreign, $5.50 No similarity between any of the names, characters, persons, and/or institutions in this magazine with those of any living or dead person or institution is intended, and any such similarity which may exist is purely coincidental. Printed in the U.S.A.

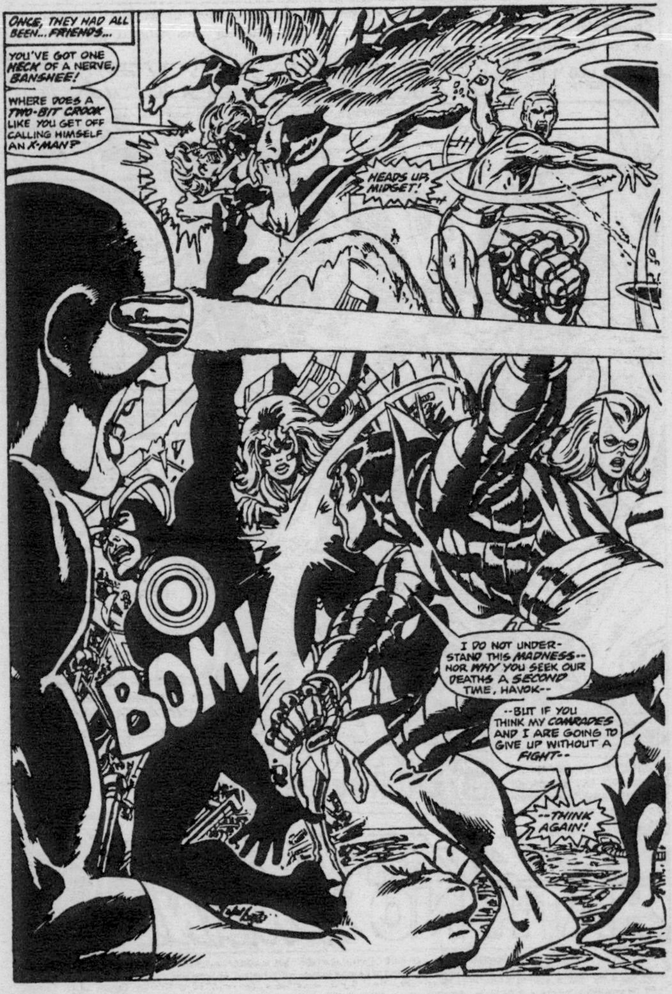
ONCE, THEY HAD ALL BEEN... FRIENDS...
YOU'VE GOT ONE HECK OF A NERVE, BANSHEE!
WHERE DOES A TWO-BIT CROOK LIKE YOU GET OFF CALLING HIMSELF AN X-MAN?
HEADS UP, MIDGET!
BOM!
I DO NOT UNDERSTAND THIS MADNESS-- NOR WHY YOU SEEK OUR DEATHS A SECOND TIME, HAVOK--
--BUT IF YOU THINK MY COMRADES AND I ARE GOING TO GIVE UP WITHOUT A FIGHT--
--THINK AGAIN!

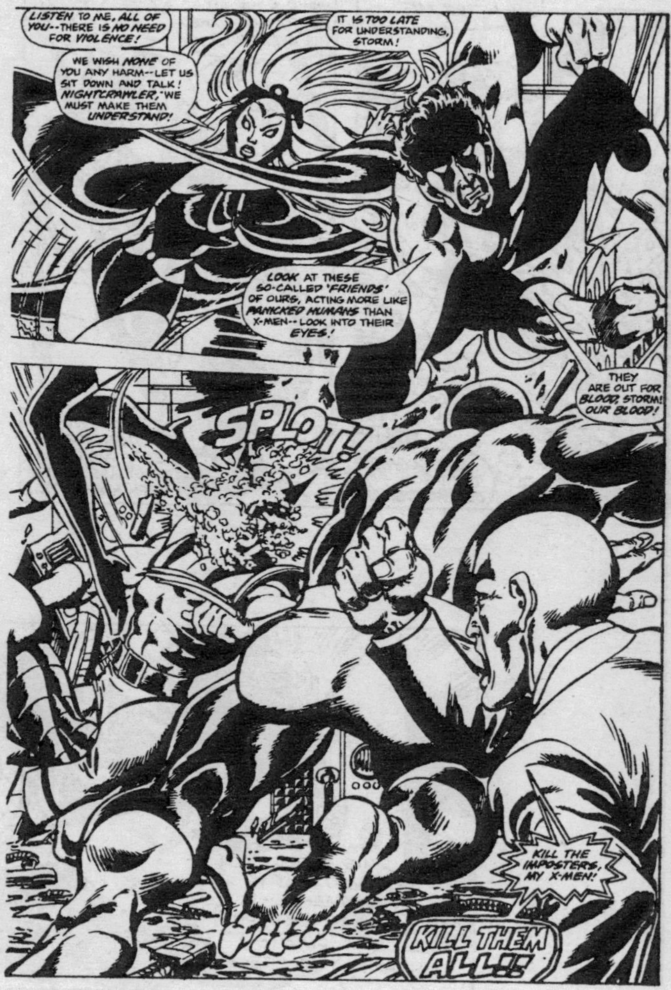
LISTEN TO ME, ALL OF YOU--THERE IS NO NEED FOR VIOLENCE!
WE WISH NONE OF YOU ANY HARM--LET US SIT DOWN AND TALK! NIGHTCRAWLER, WE MUST MAKE THEM UNDERSTAND!
IT IS TOO LATE FOR UNDERSTANDING, STORM!
LOOK AT THESE SO-CALLED 'FRIENDS' OF OURS, ACTING MORE LIKE PANICKED HUMANS THAN X-MEN--LOOK INTO THEIR EYES!
THEY ARE OUT FOR BLOOD, STORM! OUR BLOOD!
SPLOT!
KILL THE IMPOSTERS, MY X-MEN!
KILL THEM ALL!!

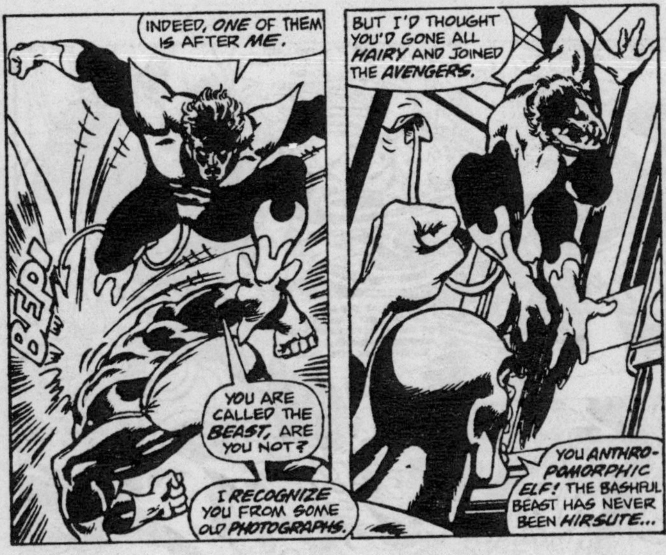
INDEED, ONE OF THEM IS AFTER ME.
YOU ARE CALLED THE BEAST, ARE YOU NOT?
I RECOGNIZE YOU FROM SOME OLD PHOTOGRAPHS.
BUT I'D THOUGHT YOU'D GONE ALL HAIRY AND JOINED THE AVENGERS.
YOU ANTHROPOMORPHIC ELF! THE BASHFUL BEAST HAS NEVER BEEN HIRSUTE...

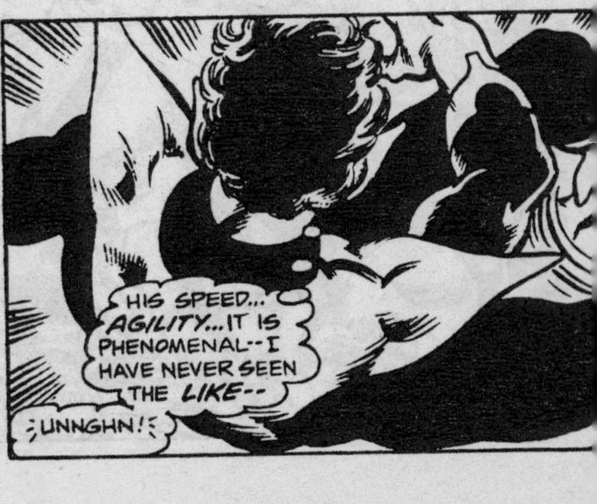
HIS SPEED... AGILITY... IT IS PHENOMENAL-- I HAVE NEVER SEEN THE LIKE--
UNNGHN!

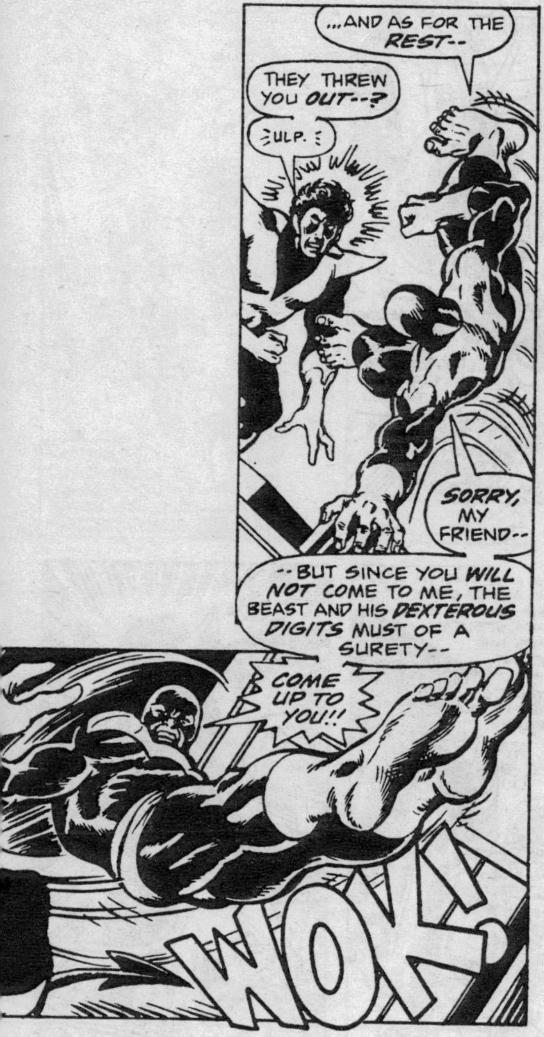
...AND AS FOR THE REST--
THEY THREW YOU OUT--?
ULP.
SORRY, MY FRIEND--
--BUT SINCE YOU WILL NOT COME TO ME, THE BEAST AND HIS DEXTEROUS DIGITS MUST OF A SURETY--
COME UP TO YOU!!
WOK!

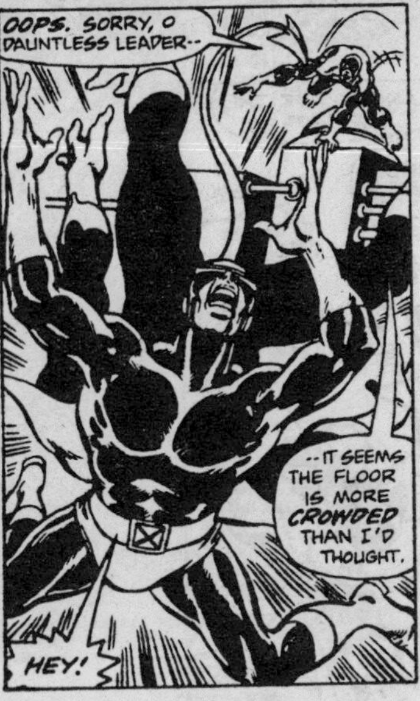
OOPS. SORRY, O DAUNTLESS LEADER--
--IT SEEMS THE FLOOR IS MORE CROWDED THAN I'D THOUGHT.
HEY!

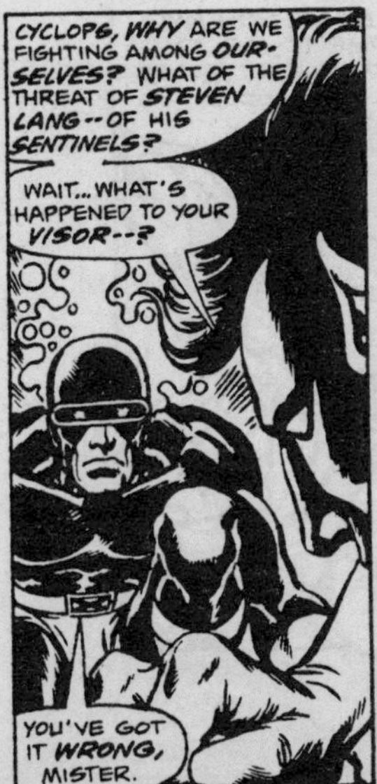
CYCLOPS, WHY ARE WE FIGHTING AMONG OURSELVES? WHAT OF THE THREAT OF STEVEN LANG--OF HIS SENTINELS?
WAIT... WHAT'S HAPPENED TO YOUR VISOR--?
YOU'VE GOT IT WRONG, MISTER.

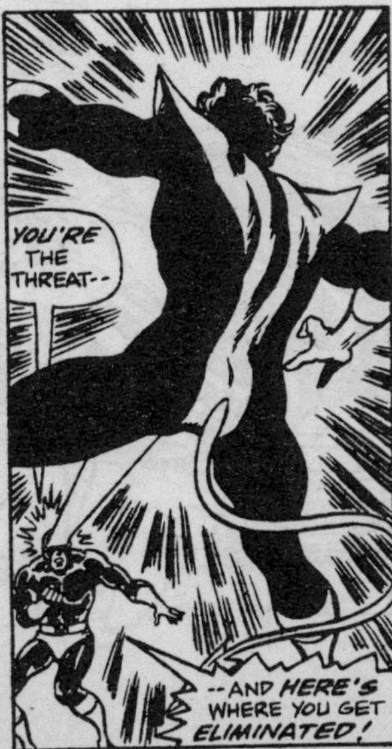
YOU'RE THE THREAT--
--AND HERE'S WHERE YOU GET ELIMINATED!

THAT LITTLE STUNT IS ALL SHE WROTE, PAL!

AND IF YOU'RE WONDERING WHICH X-MAN HAS THE *PLEASURE* OF *BLASTING* YOU FROM HERE TO *HADES*, ALL YOU HAVE TO DO IS--

--CRY *HAVOK!*

I...*KNOW* WHO YOU ARE...*ASSASSIN!*

SUCH POWER--I NEVER *DREAMED*--WERE I *HUMAN*, THAT BLAST WOULD HAVE *BURNED* ME TO A *CRISP.*

BUT EVEN MY *ARMORED* BODY HAS ITS *LIMITS*--BY ALL THAT I HOLD *DEAR*, HE IS CAUSING ME-- *PAIN!!*

I CANNOT STAND MUCH *MORE* OF THIS.

BUT I *WILL*...STAND, I WILL--I *MUST*--SURVIVE!

*HEAR* ME, *HAVOK*--*COLOSSUS* IS COMING FOR YOU--

--AND--I--*WILL*--NOT--BE-- *STOPPED!*

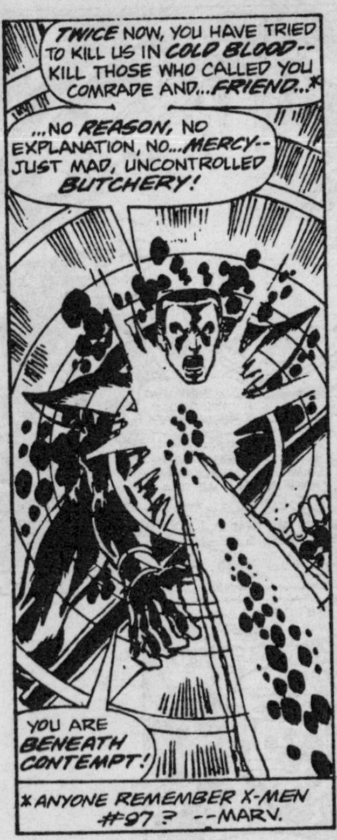
TWICE NOW, YOU HAVE TRIED TO KILL US IN COLD BLOOD-- KILL THOSE WHO CALLED YOU COMRADE AND...FRIEND...*
...NO REASON, NO EXPLANATION, NO...MERCY-- JUST MAD, UNCONTROLLED BUTCHERY!
YOU ARE BENEATH CONTEMPT!
*ANYONE REMEMBER X-MEN #97? --MARV.

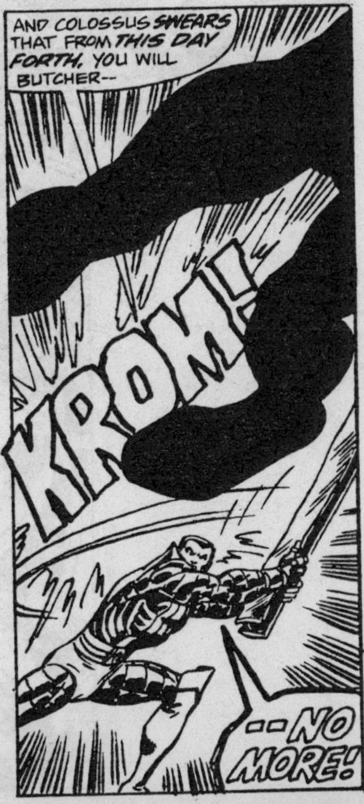
AND COLOSSUS SWEARS THAT FROM THIS DAY FORTH, YOU WILL BUTCHER--
KROM!
--NO MORE!

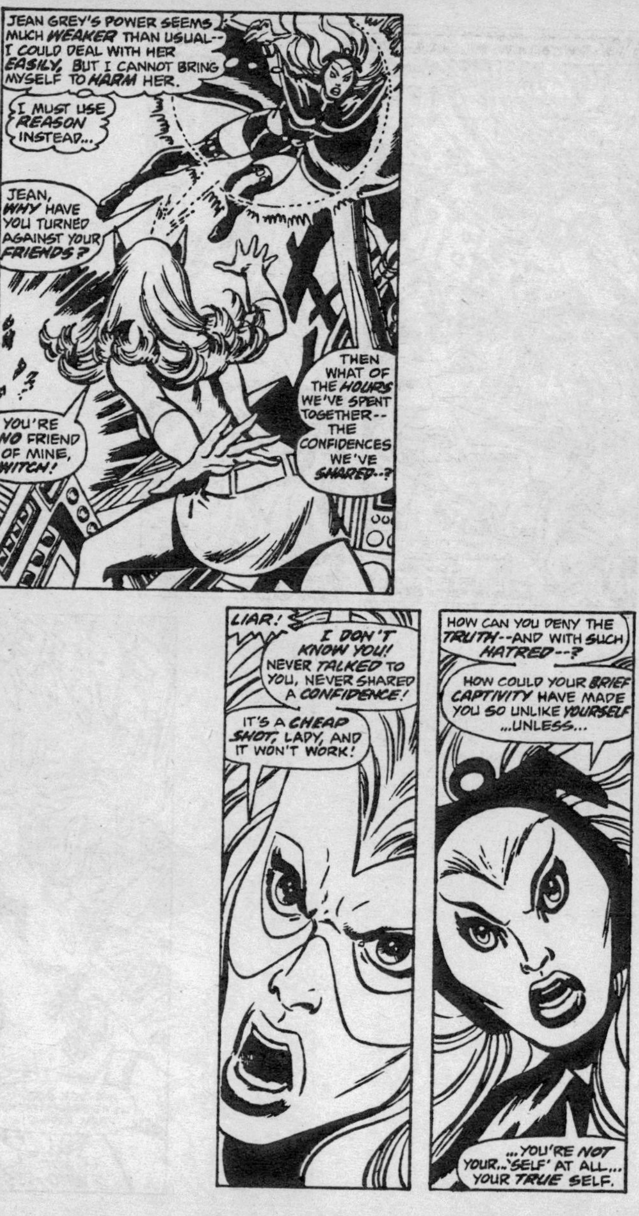

JEAN GREY'S POWER SEEMS MUCH WEAKER THAN USUAL-- I COULD DEAL WITH HER EASILY, BUT I CANNOT BRING MYSELF TO HARM HER.
I MUST USE REASON INSTEAD...
JEAN, WHY HAVE YOU TURNED AGAINST YOUR FRIENDS?
YOU'RE NO FRIEND OF MINE, WITCH!
THEN WHAT OF THE HOURS WE'VE SPENT TOGETHER-- THE CONFIDENCES WE'VE SHARED--?
LIAR!
I DON'T KNOW YOU! NEVER TALKED TO YOU, NEVER SHARED A CONFIDENCE!
IT'S A CHEAP SHOT, LADY, AND IT WON'T WORK!
HOW CAN YOU DENY THE TRUTH--AND WITH SUCH HATRED--?
HOW COULD YOUR BRIEF CAPTIVITY HAVE MADE YOU SO UNLIKE YOURSELF ...UNLESS...
...YOU'RE NOT YOUR...'SELF' AT ALL... YOUR TRUE SELF.

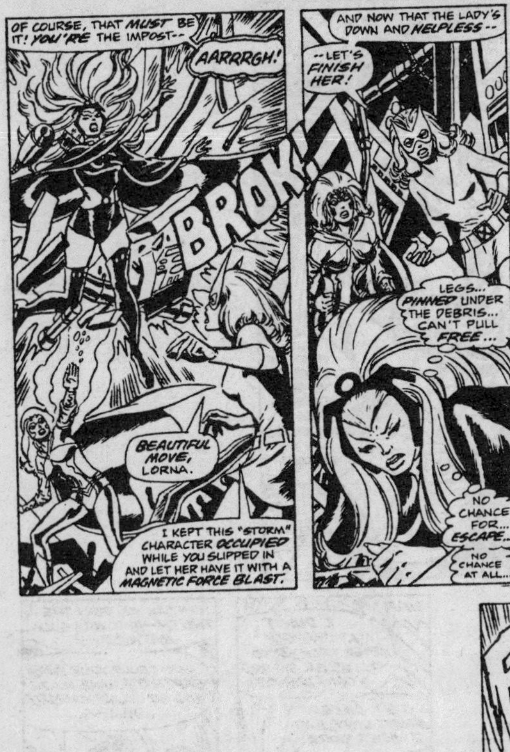
OF COURSE, THAT MUST BE IT! YOU'RE THE IMPOST--
AARRRGH!
BROK!
I KEPT THIS "STORM" CHARACTER OCCUPIED WHILE YOU SLIPPED IN AND LET HER HAVE IT WITH A MAGNETIC FORCE BLAST.
BEAUTIFUL MOVE, LORNA.
AND NOW THAT THE LADY'S DOWN AND HELPLESS--
--LET'S FINISH HER!
LEGS... PINNED UNDER THE DEBRIS... CAN'T PULL FREE...
NO CHANCE FOR... ESCAPE...
NO CHANCE AT ALL...

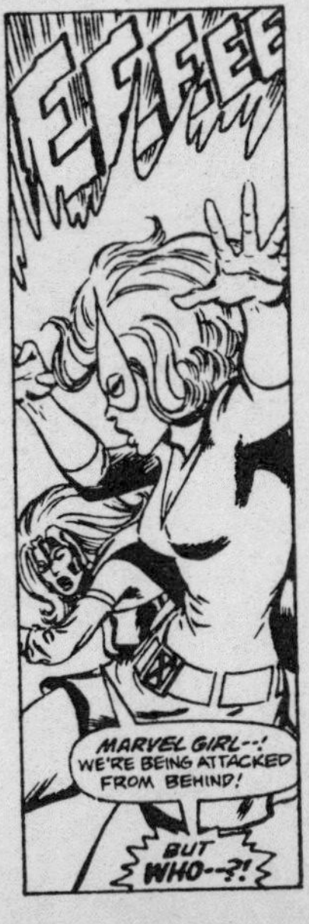
EEFFEE
MARVEL GIRL--! WE'RE BEING ATTACKED FROM BEHIND!
BUT WHO--?!

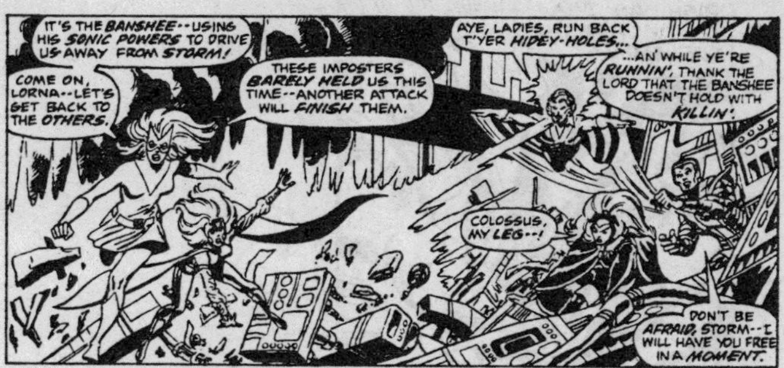
IT'S THE BANSHEE--USING HIS SONIC POWERS TO DRIVE US AWAY FROM STORM!
COME ON, LORNA--LET'S GET BACK TO THE OTHERS.
THESE IMPOSTERS BARELY HELD US THIS TIME--ANOTHER ATTACK WILL FINISH THEM.
AYE, LADIES, RUN BACK T'YER HIDEY-HOLES...
...AN' WHILE YE'RE RUNNIN', THANK THE LORD THAT THE BANSHEE DOESN'T HOLD WITH KILLIN'.
COLOSSUS, MY LEG--!
DON'T BE AFRAID, STORM--I WILL HAVE YOU FREE IN A MOMENT.

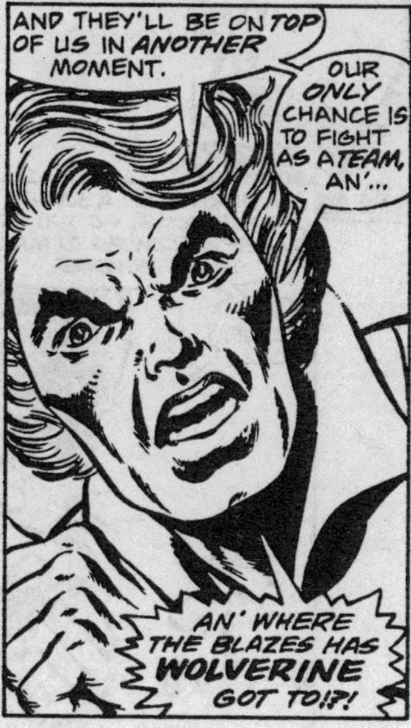
AND THEY'LL BE ON TOP OF US IN ANOTHER MOMENT.
OUR ONLY CHANCE IS TO FIGHT AS A TEAM, AN'...
AN' WHERE THE BLAZES HAS WOLVERINE GOT TO!?!

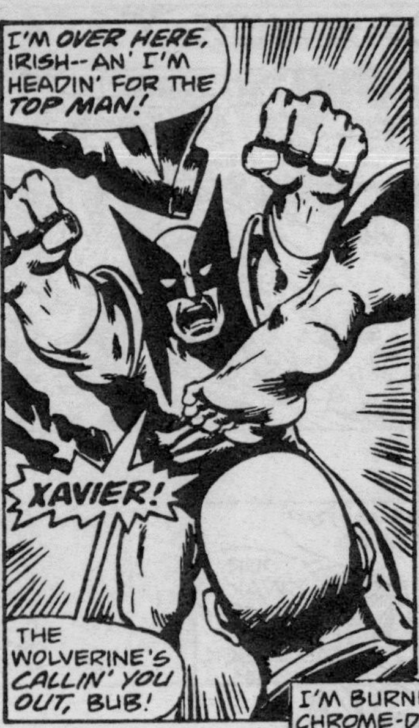
I'M OVER HERE, IRISH--AN' I'M HEADIN' FOR THE TOP MAN!
XAVIER!
THE WOLVERINE'S CALLIN' YOU OUT, BUB!

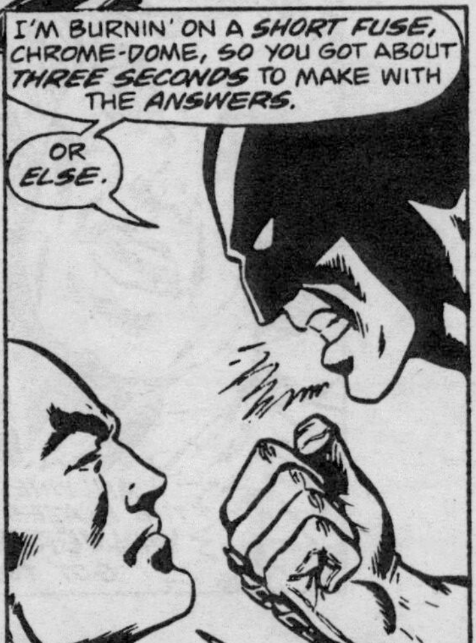
I'M BURNIN' ON A SHORT FUSE, CHROME-DOME, SO YOU GOT ABOUT THREE SECONDS TO MAKE WITH THE ANSWERS.
OR ELSE.
YOUR THREATS DO NOT IMPRESS ME, WOLVERINE.

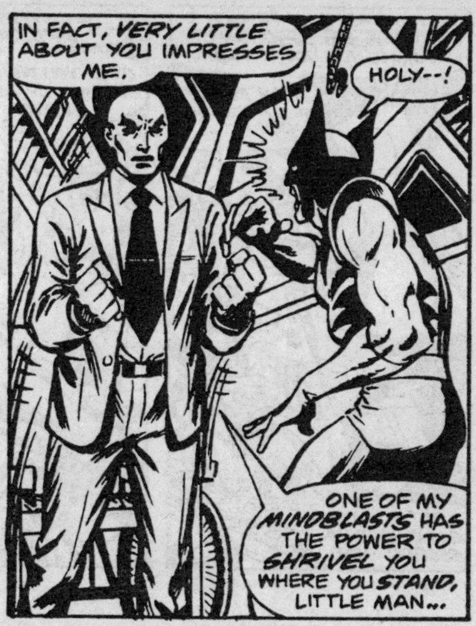
IN FACT, VERY LITTLE ABOUT YOU IMPRESSES ME.
HOLY--!
ONE OF MY MINDBLASTS HAS THE POWER TO SHRIVEL YOU WHERE YOU STAND, LITTLE MAN...

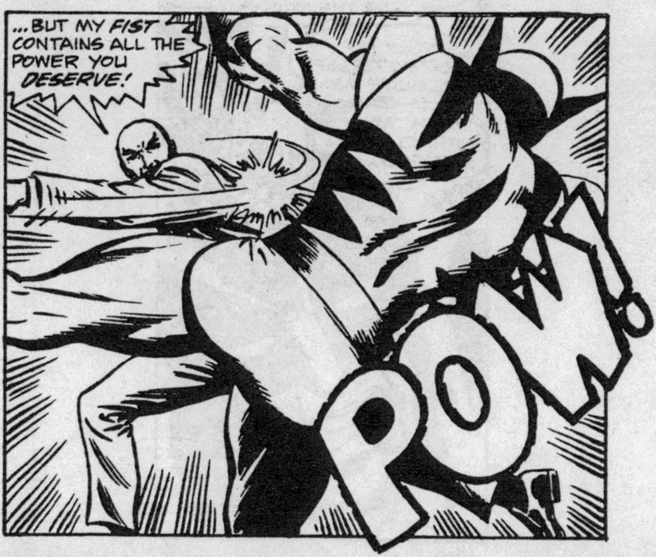
...BUT MY FIST CONTAINS ALL THE POWER YOU DESERVE!
POW!

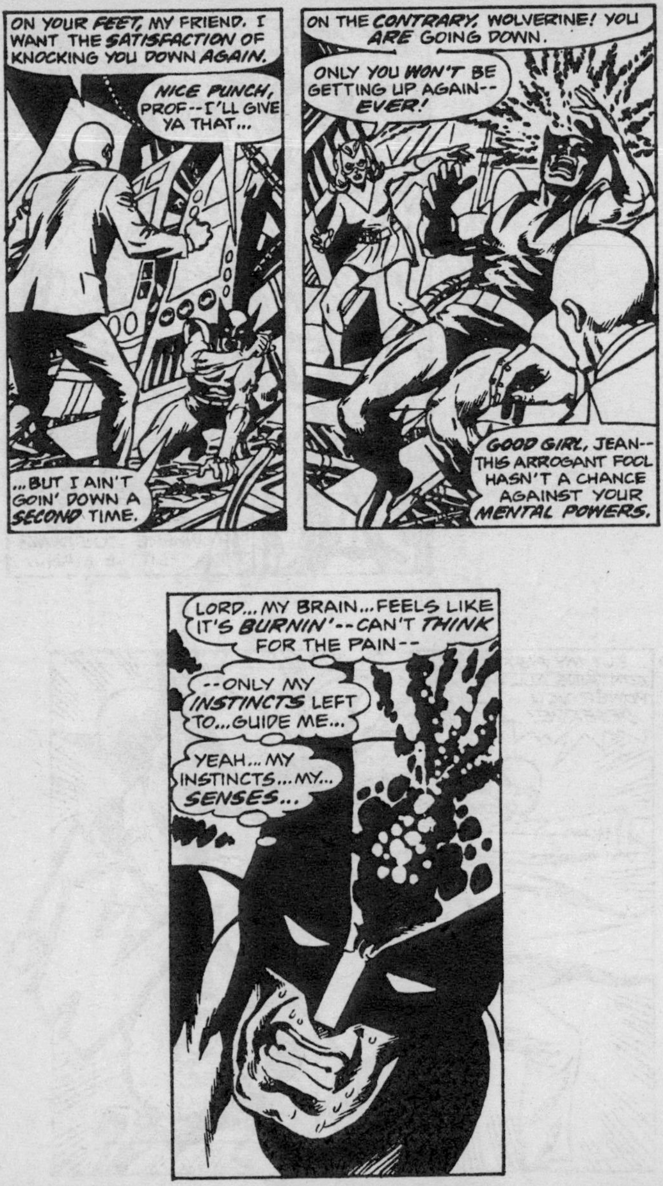
ON YOUR FEET, MY FRIEND. I WANT THE SATISFACTION OF KNOCKING YOU DOWN AGAIN.
NICE PUNCH, PROF--I'LL GIVE YA THAT...
...BUT I AIN'T GOIN' DOWN A SECOND TIME.
ON THE CONTRARY, WOLVERINE! YOU ARE GOING DOWN.
ONLY YOU WON'T BE GETTING UP AGAIN-- EVER!
GOOD GIRL, JEAN-- THIS ARROGANT FOOL HASN'T A CHANCE AGAINST YOUR MENTAL POWERS.
LORD... MY BRAIN... FEELS LIKE IT'S BURNIN'--CAN'T THINK FOR THE PAIN--
--ONLY MY INSTINCTS LEFT TO... GUIDE ME...
YEAH... MY INSTINCTS... MY... SENSES...

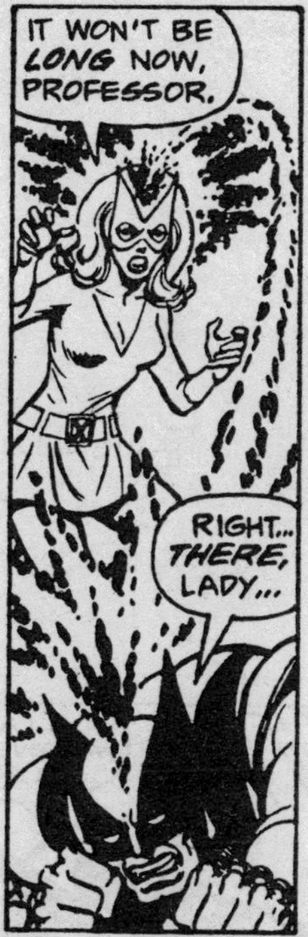
IT WON'T BE LONG NOW, PROFESSOR.
RIGHT... THERE, LADY...

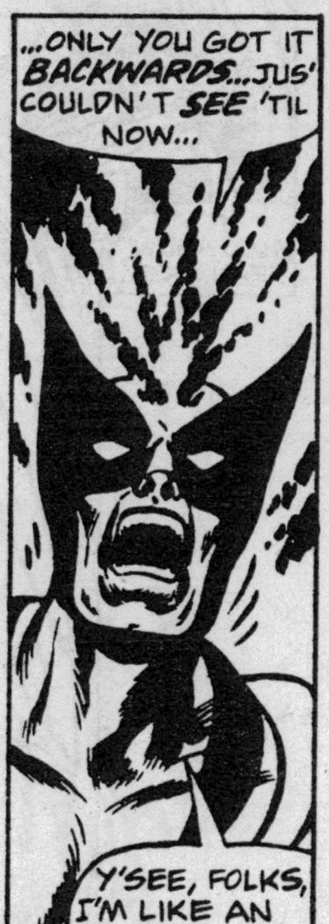
...ONLY YOU GOT IT BACKWARDS...JUS' COULDN'T SEE 'TIL NOW...
Y'SEE, FOLKS, I'M LIKE AN ANIMAL--

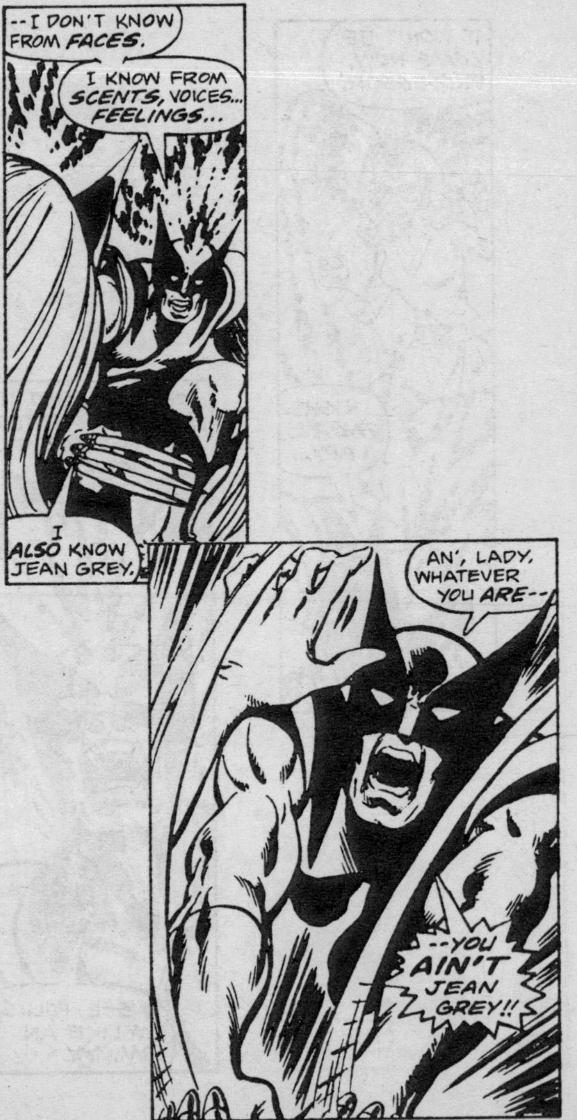
--I DON'T KNOW FROM FACES.
I KNOW FROM SCENTS, VOICES... FEELINGS...
I ALSO KNOW JEAN GREY.
AN', LADY, WHATEVER YOU ARE--
--YOU AIN'T JEAN GREY!!

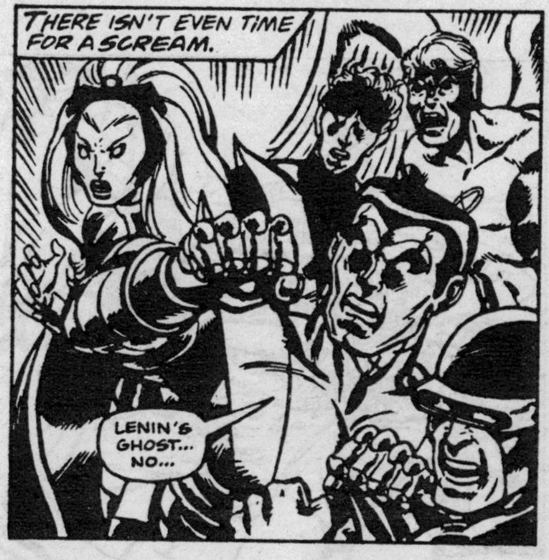
THERE ISN'T EVEN TIME FOR A SCREAM.
LENIN'S GHOST... NO...

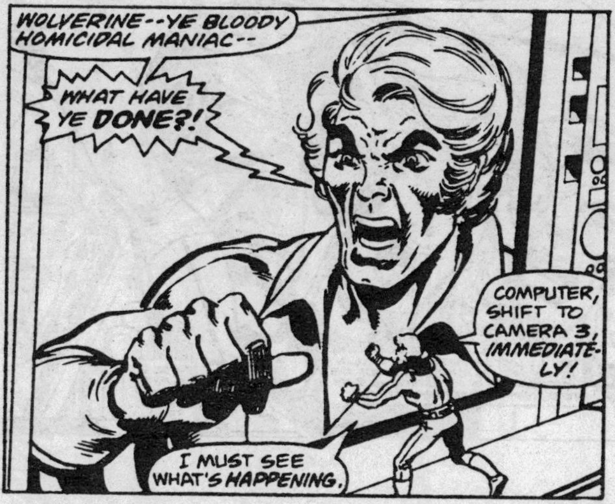
WOLVERINE--YE BLOODY HOMICIDAL MANIAC--
WHAT HAVE YE DONE?!
COMPUTER, SHIFT TO CAMERA 3, IMMEDIATE-LY!
I MUST SEE WHAT'S HAPPENING.

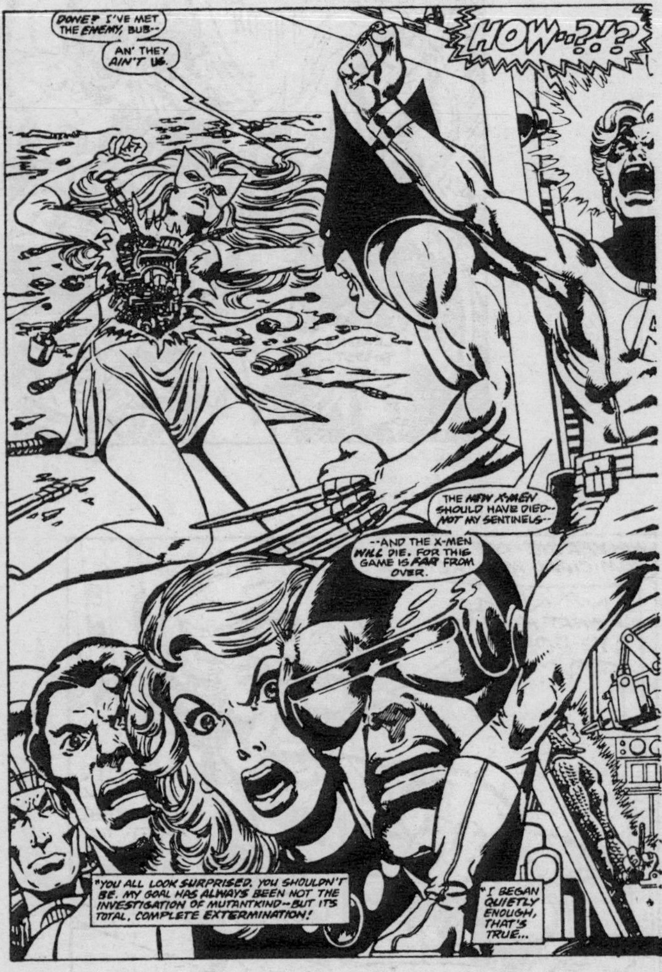

DONE? I'VE MET THE ENEMY, BUB--
AN' THEY AIN'T US.
HOW..?!?
THE NEW X-MEN SHOULD HAVE DIED-- NOT MY SENTINELS--
--AND THE X-MEN WILL DIE. FOR THIS GAME IS FAR FROM OVER.
"YOU ALL LOOK SURPRISED. YOU SHOULDN'T BE. MY GOAL HAS ALWAYS BEEN NOT THE INVESTIGATION OF MUTANTKIND--BUT ITS TOTAL, COMPLETE EXTERMINATION!
"I BEGAN QUIETLY ENOUGH, THAT'S TRUE...

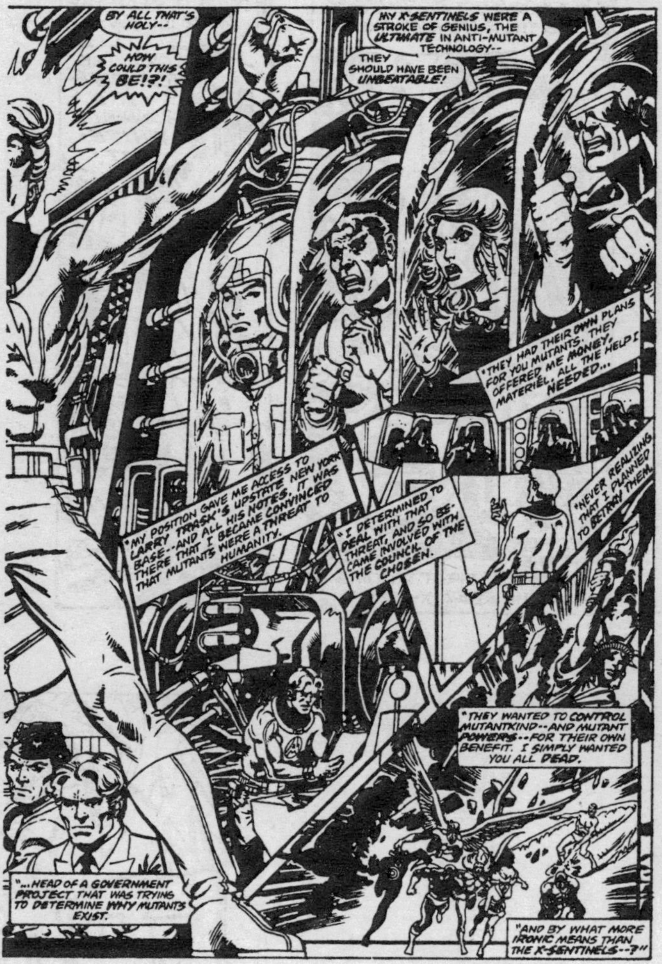
BY ALL THAT'S HOLY--
HOW COULD THIS BE!?!
MY X-SENTINELS WERE A STROKE OF GENIUS, THE ULTIMATE IN ANTI-MUTANT TECHNOLOGY--
THEY SHOULD HAVE BEEN UNBEATABLE!
"...HEAD OF A GOVERNMENT PROJECT THAT WAS TRYING TO DETERMINE WHY MUTANTS EXIST.
"MY POSITION GAVE ME ACCESS TO LARRY TRASK'S UPSTATE NEW YORK BASE--AND ALL HIS NOTES. IT WAS THERE THAT I BECAME CONVINCED THAT MUTANTS WERE A THREAT TO HUMANITY.
"I DETERMINED TO DEAL WITH THAT THREAT, AND SO BECAME INVOLVED WITH THE COUNCIL OF THE CHOSEN.
"THEY HAD THEIR OWN PLANS FOR YOU MUTANTS. THEY OFFERED ME MONEY, MATERIEL, ALL THE HELP I NEEDED...
"NEVER REALIZING THAT I PLANNED TO BETRAY THEM.
"THEY WANTED TO CONTROL MUTANTKIND--AND MUTANT POWERS--FOR THEIR OWN BENEFIT. I SIMPLY WANTED YOU ALL DEAD.
"AND BY WHAT MORE IRONIC MEANS THAN THE X-SENTINELS--?"

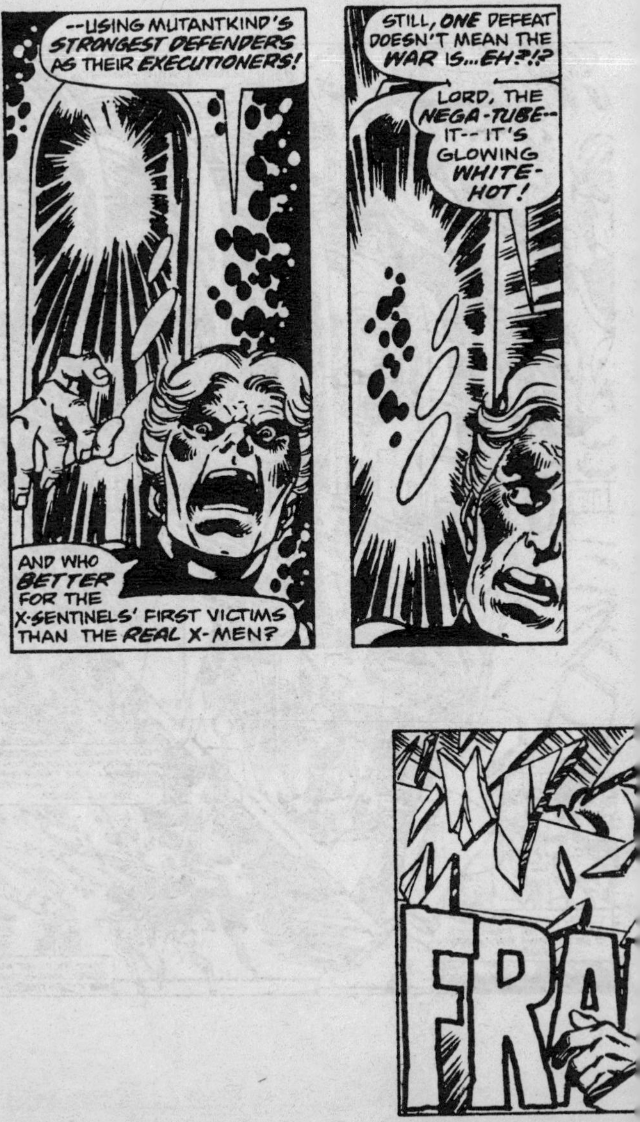
--USING MUTANTKIND'S STRONGEST DEFENDERS AS THEIR EXECUTIONERS!
AND WHO BETTER FOR THE X-SENTINELS' FIRST VICTIMS THAN THE REAL X-MEN?
STILL, ONE DEFEAT DOESN'T MEAN THE WAR IS...EH?!?
LORD, THE NEGA-TUBE-- IT-- IT'S GLOWING WHITE-HOT!
FRA

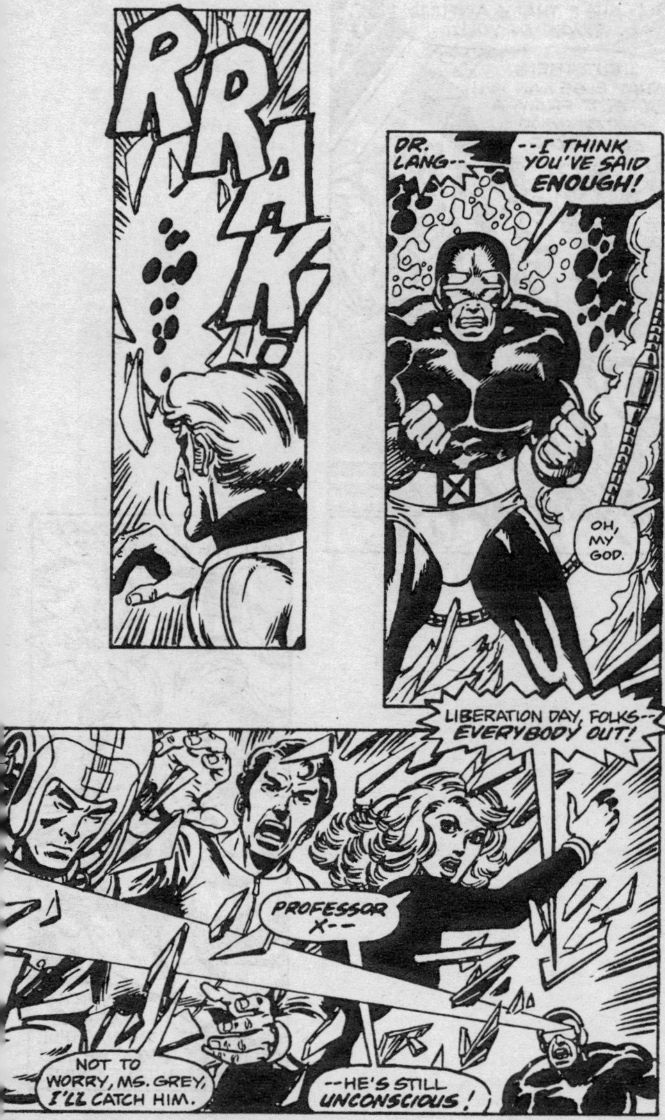
RRAK
DR. LANG--
--I THINK YOU'VE SAID ENOUGH!
OH, MY GOD.
LIBERATION DAY, FOLKS--EVERYBODY OUT!
PROFESSOR X--
--HE'S STILL UNCONSCIOUS!
NOT TO WORRY, MS. GREY, I'LL CATCH HIM.

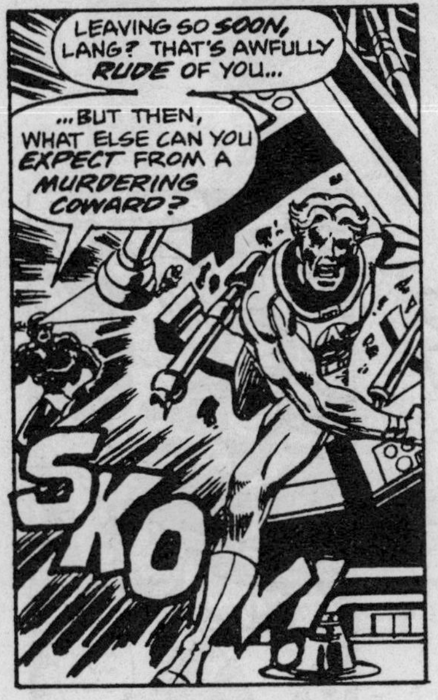
LEAVING SO SOON, LANG? THAT'S AWFULLY RUDE OF YOU...
...BUT THEN, WHAT ELSE CAN YOU EXPECT FROM A MURDERING COWARD?
SKOM!

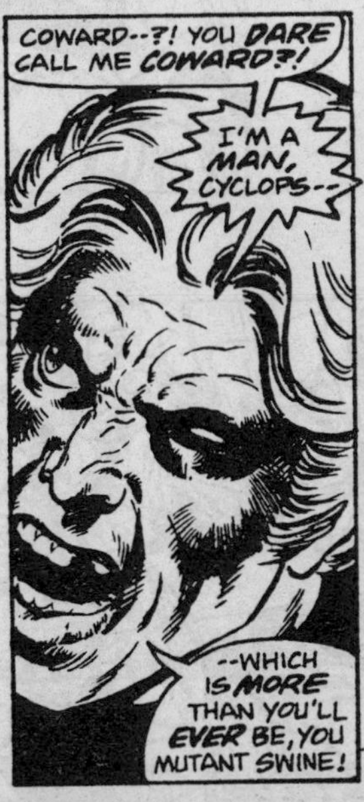
COWARD--?! YOU DARE CALL ME COWARD?!
I'M A MAN, CYCLOPS--
--WHICH IS MORE THAN YOU'LL EVER BE, YOU MUTANT SWINE!

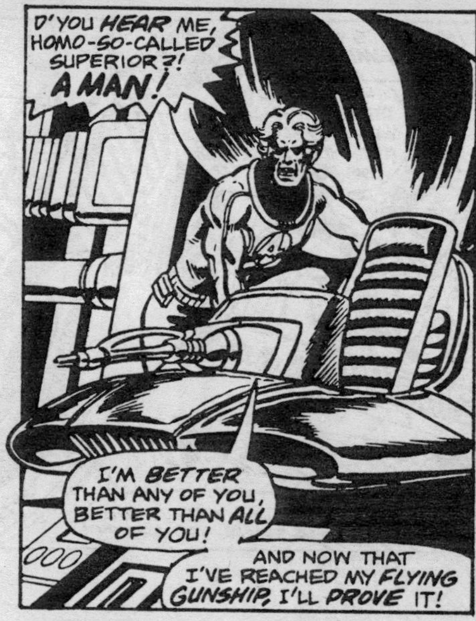
D'YOU HEAR ME, HOMO-SO-CALLED SUPERIOR?! A MAN!
I'M BETTER THAN ANY OF YOU, BETTER THAN ALL OF YOU!
AND NOW THAT I'VE REACHED MY FLYING GUNSHIP, I'LL PROVE IT!

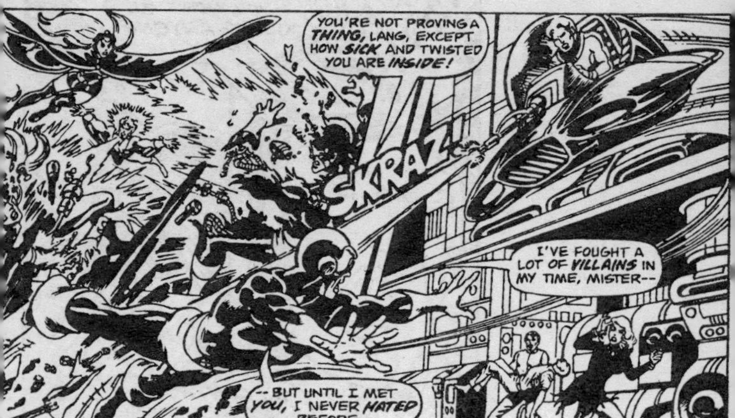
YOU'RE NOT PROVING A THING, LANG, EXCEPT HOW SICK AND TWISTED YOU ARE INSIDE!
SKRAZ!
I'VE FOUGHT A LOT OF VILLAINS IN MY TIME, MISTER--
--BUT UNTIL I MET YOU, I NEVER HATED BEFORE.

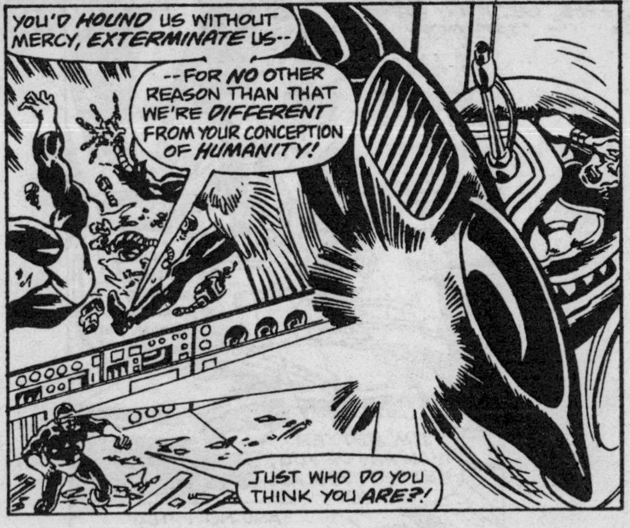
YOU'D HOUND US WITHOUT MERCY, EXTERMINATE US--
--FOR NO OTHER REASON THAN THAT WE'RE DIFFERENT FROM YOUR CONCEPTION OF HUMANITY!
JUST WHO DO YOU THINK YOU ARE?!

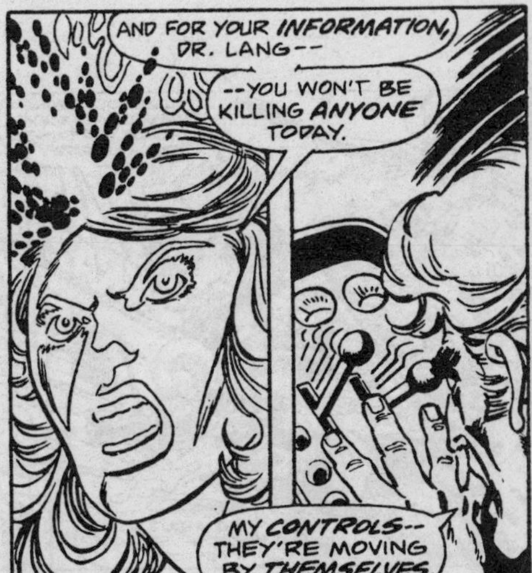
AND FOR YOUR INFORMATION, DR. LANG--
--YOU WON'T BE KILLING ANYONE TODAY.
MY CONTROLS-- THEY'RE MOVING BY THEMSELVES.

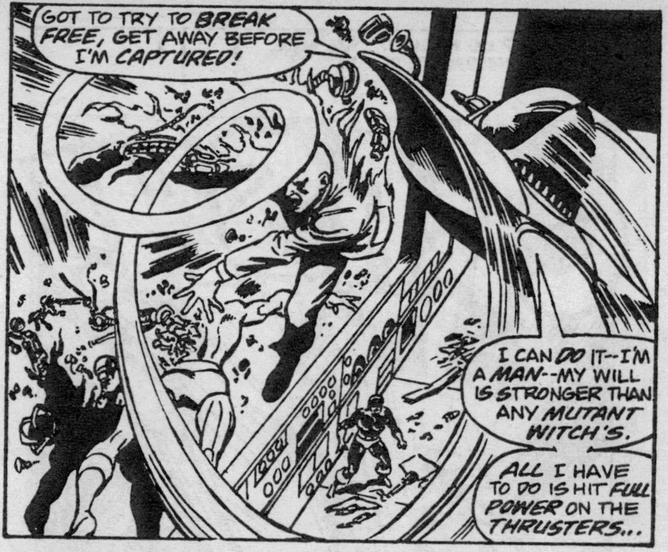
GOT TO TRY TO BREAK FREE, GET AWAY BEFORE I'M CAPTURED!
I CAN DO IT--I'M A MAN--MY WILL IS STRONGER THAN ANY MUTANT WITCH'S.
ALL I HAVE TO DO IS HIT FULL POWER ON THE THRUSTERS...

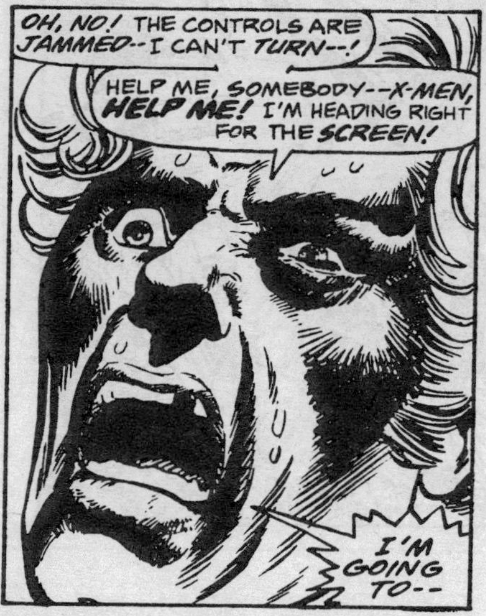
OH, NO! THE CONTROLS ARE JAMMED--I CAN'T TURN--!
HELP ME, SOMEBODY--X-MEN, HELP ME! I'M HEADING RIGHT FOR THE SCREEN!
I'M GOING TO--

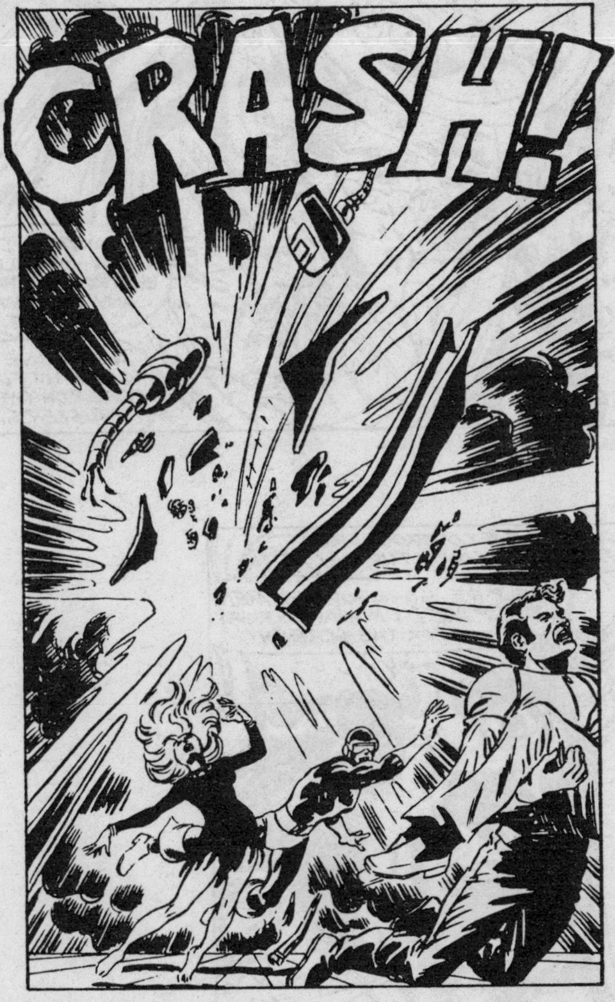
CRASH!

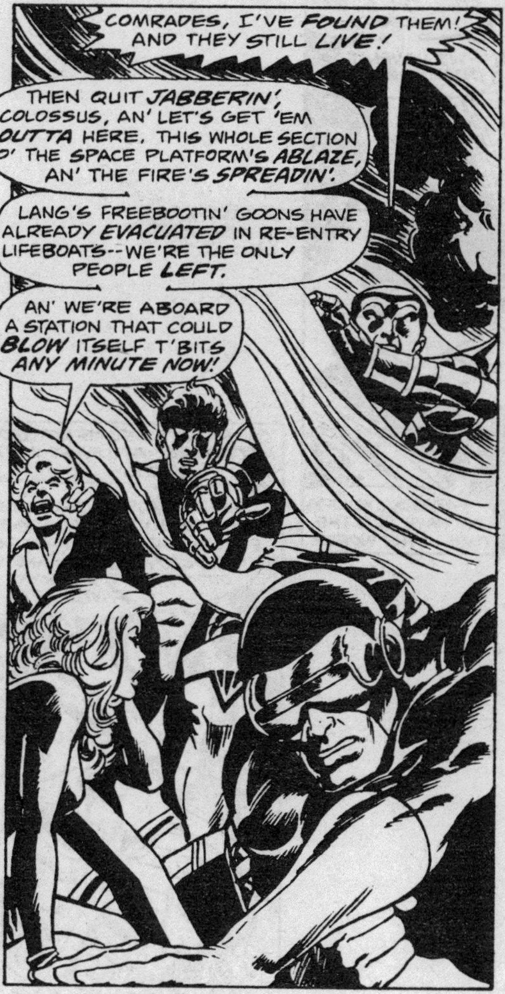
COMRADES, I'VE FOUND THEM! AND THEY STILL LIVE!
THEN QUIT JABBERIN', COLOSSUS, AN' LET'S GET 'EM OUTTA HERE. THIS WHOLE SECTION O' THE SPACE PLATFORM'S ABLAZE, AN' THE FIRE'S SPREADIN'.
LANG'S FREEBOOTIN' GOONS HAVE ALREADY EVACUATED IN RE-ENTRY LIFEBOATS--WE'RE THE ONLY PEOPLE LEFT.
AN' WE'RE ABOARD A STATION THAT COULD BLOW ITSELF T'BITS ANY MINUTE NOW!

A FEW MINUTES LATER...

THE FIRE'S ALMOST REACHED THE *HYPERGOLIC* FUEL CELLS, DR. CORBEAU--

--WE HAVEN'T MUCH *TIME.*

WRONG, CYCLOPS, WE HAVE *ALL* THE TIME IN THE WORLD.

'CAUSE WE'RE SURE NOT *GOING* ANYWHERE--AT LEAST IN *THIS* CRATE.

THE *FLIGHT CONTROL COMPUTER* MUST'VE GOTTEN SLAGGED DURING OUR LITTLE *FRACAS* WITH THE *SENTINELS**--AND WITH-OUT IT, WE'RE AS GOOD AS *FINISHED.*

WHAT ABOUT A *MANUAL* RE-ENTRY?

*LAST ISH. --MARV.

WHAT *ABOUT* IT, WOLVERINE?

IN CASE YOU HADN'T *NOTICED*...

...WE'VE GOT A THUMPING GREAT *HOLE* IN THE SHUTTLE'S HULL, AND--THANKS AGAIN TO THE SENTINELS--NO FUNCTIONAL *PRESSURE SUITS*.

BUT THAT'S THE *LEAST* OF OUR PROBLEMS.

ICH...VERST'HEN, *HERR DOKTOR*... ...THE *SOLAR FLARE*.

YOU GOT IT, NIGHTCRAWLER. THE *WORST* FLARE IN YEARS. THE *COMPUTER* WAS SUPPOSED TO FLY US THROUGH IT WHILE WE SAT *SAFE-AND-SOUND* IN THE SHUTTLE'S SHIELDED *'LIFE-CELL.'*

ONLY WE HAVE *NO* COMPUTER.

SURE, I CAN FLY A RE-ENTRY, *NO SWEAT*, BUT I WOULDN'T LAST *THIRTY SECONDS* IN THAT FLARE.

ONE OF *YOU* MIGHT *SURVIVE* THE FLARE, BUT YOU CAN'T *PILOT* THE SHUTTLE WE NEED SOMEONE WHO CAN DO *BOTH*, AND THERE'S *NO SUCH ANIMAL*.

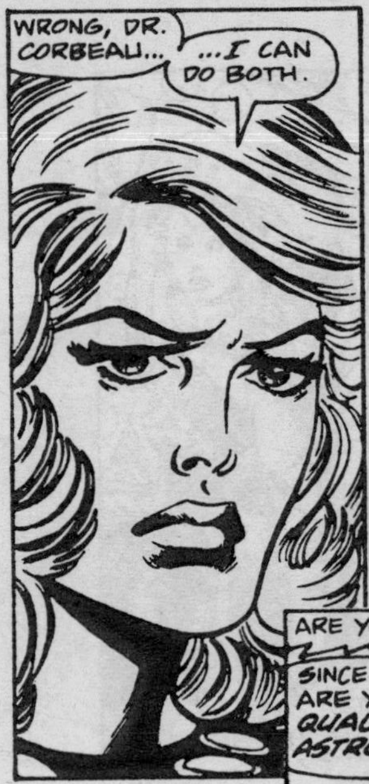
WRONG, DR. CORBEAU...
...I CAN DO BOTH.

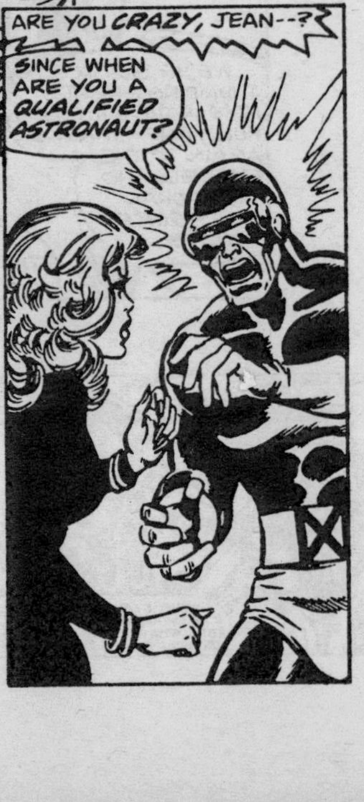
ARE YOU CRAZY, JEAN--?
SINCE WHEN ARE YOU A QUALIFIED ASTRONAUT?

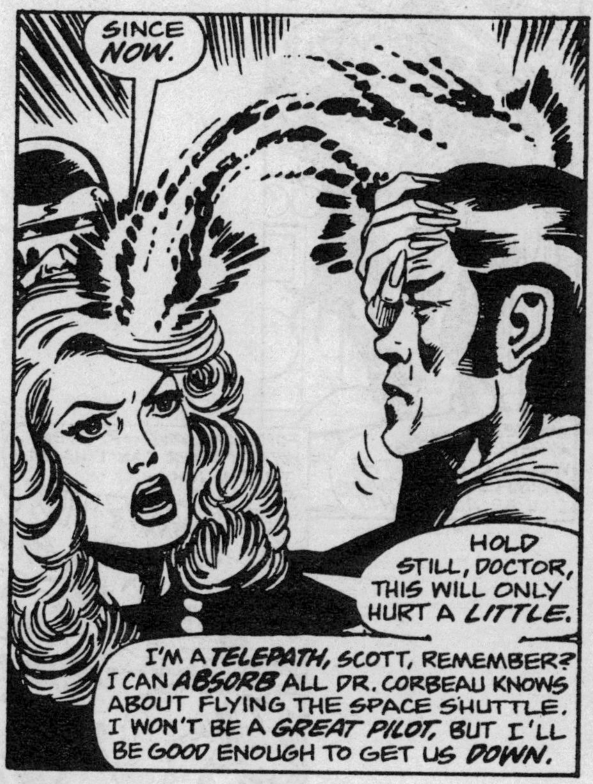
SINCE NOW.
HOLD STILL, DOCTOR, THIS WILL ONLY HURT A LITTLE.
I'M A TELEPATH, SCOTT, REMEMBER? I CAN ABSORB ALL DR. CORBEAU KNOWS ABOUT FLYING THE SPACE SHUTTLE. I WON'T BE A GREAT PILOT, BUT I'LL BE GOOD ENOUGH TO GET US DOWN.

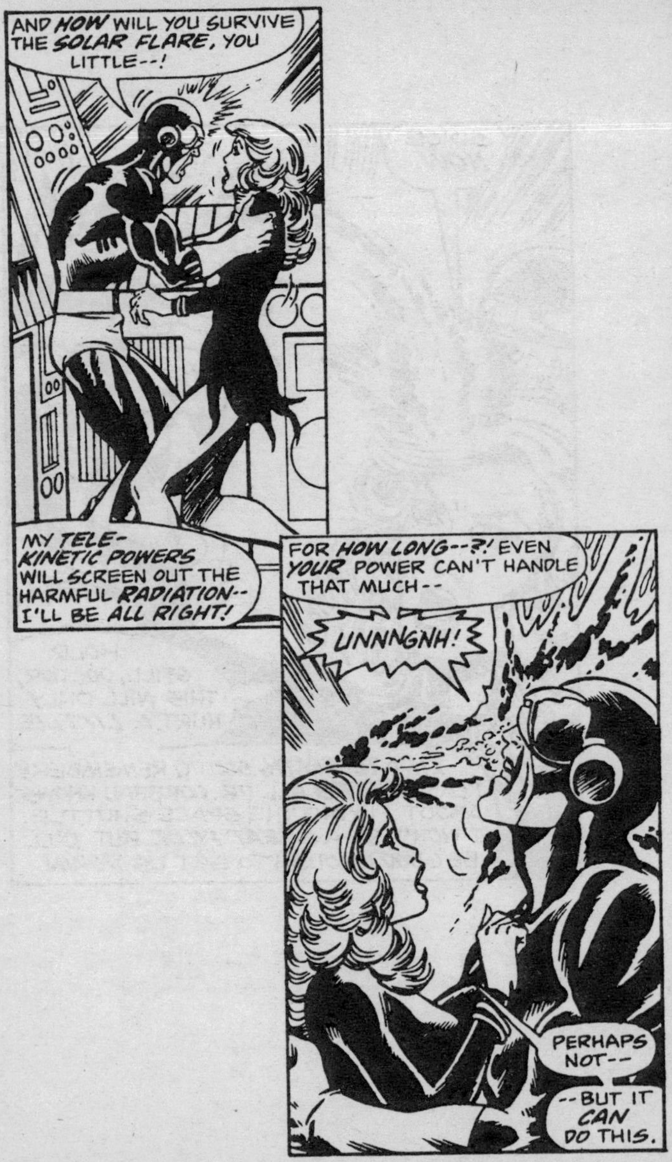
AND HOW WILL YOU SURVIVE THE SOLAR FLARE, YOU LITTLE--!
MY TELE-KINETIC POWERS WILL SCREEN OUT THE HARMFUL RADIATION--I'LL BE ALL RIGHT!
FOR HOW LONG--?! EVEN YOUR POWER CAN'T HANDLE THAT MUCH--
UNNNGNH!
PERHAPS NOT--
--BUT IT CAN DO THIS.

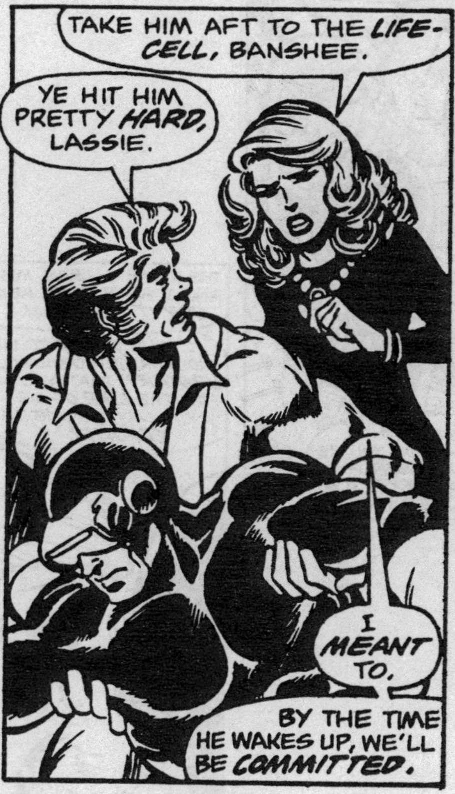
TAKE HIM AFT TO THE LIFE-CELL, BANSHEE.
YE HIT HIM PRETTY HARD, LASSIE.
I MEANT TO.
BY THE TIME HE WAKES UP, WE'LL BE COMMITTED.

NICE SHOT, LADY--YOU BUCKIN' FOR *MARTYR O' THE YEAR* OR SOMETHIN'?

MAKE IT QUICK, WOLVERINE--I'M *BUSY.*

WHAT'RE YA TRYIN' TA *PROVE*--THAT YOU'RE AS *GOOD AN' NOBLE* AS *BIG DADDY X?* IT'S *SUICIDE,* JEANNIE!

THE NAME IS *JEAN,* MISTER-- AND I HAVE JUST ABOUT *HAD IT* WITH YOU!

I HAVE *TRIED* TO LIKE YOU, WOLVERINE--OBNOXIOUS LITTLE *UPSTART* THAT YOU ARE--BUT FOR THE *LIFE* OF ME, I DON'T KNOW WHY I MADE THE *EFFORT!*

SO SHUT YOUR *MOUTH,* AND GET INTO THE LIFE CELL--*NOW!* --BEFORE I LOSE MY *TEMPER!*

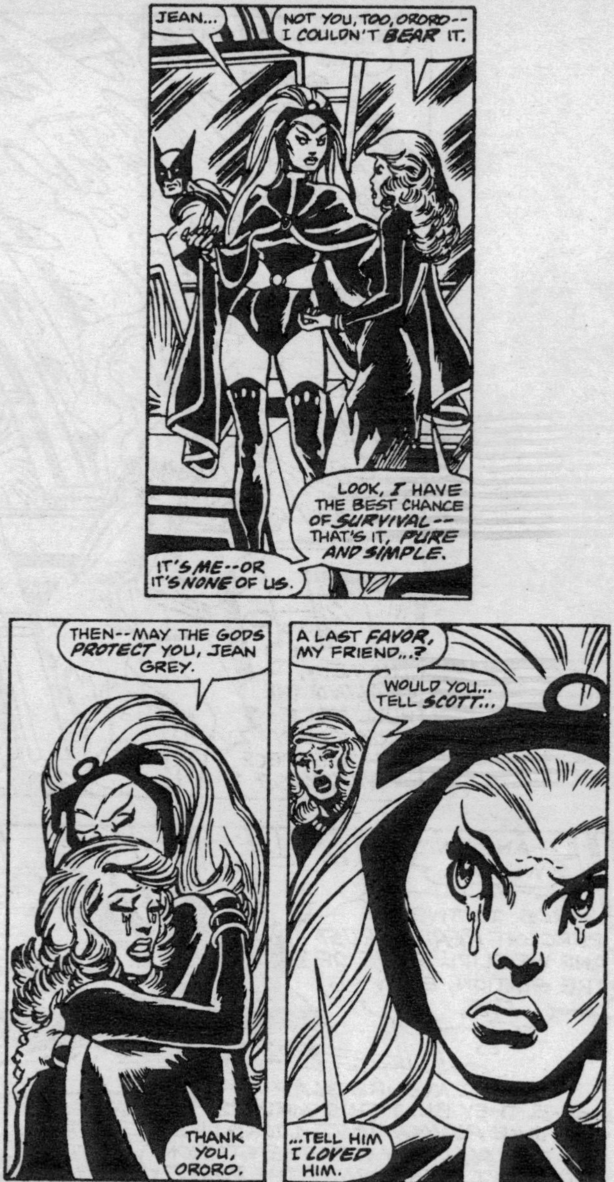
JEAN...
NOT YOU, TOO, ORORO-- I COULDN'T BEAR IT.
LOOK, I HAVE THE BEST CHANCE OF SURVIVAL-- THAT'S IT, PURE AND SIMPLE.
IT'S ME--OR IT'S NONE OF US.
THEN--MAY THE GODS PROTECT YOU, JEAN GREY.
THANK YOU, ORORO.
A LAST FAVOR, MY FRIEND...?
WOULD YOU... TELL SCOTT...
...TELL HIM I LOVED HIM.

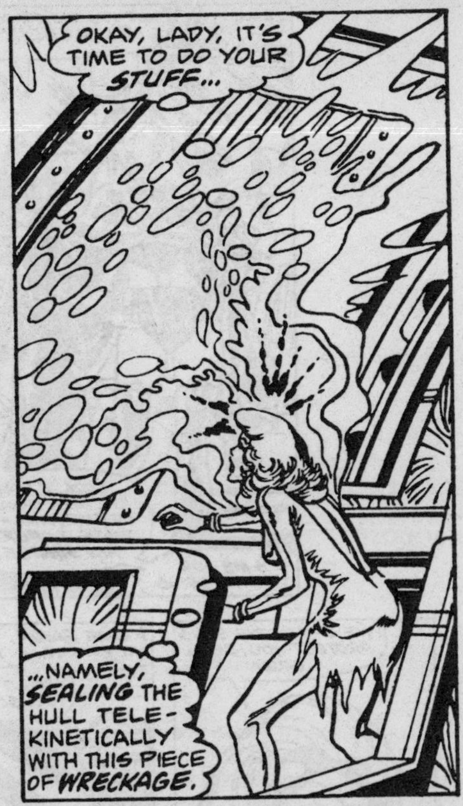
OKAY, LADY, IT'S TIME TO DO YOUR STUFF...
...NAMELY, SEALING THE HULL TELE-KINETICALLY WITH THIS PIECE OF WRECKAGE.

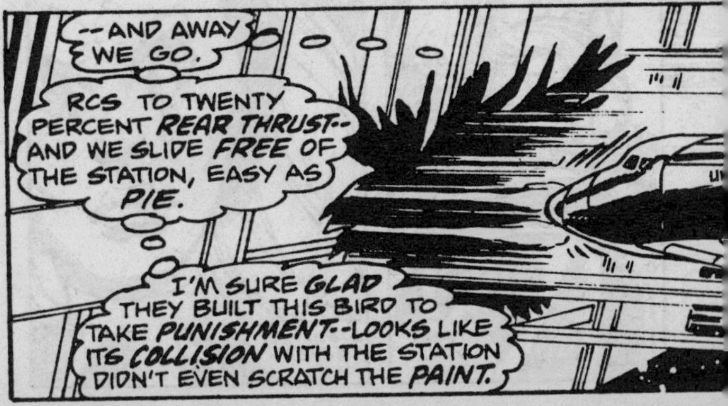
--AND AWAY WE GO.
RCS TO TWENTY PERCENT REAR THRUST--AND WE SLIDE FREE OF THE STATION, EASY AS PIE.
I'M SURE GLAD THEY BUILT THIS BIRD TO TAKE PUNISHMENT--LOOKS LIKE ITS COLLISION WITH THE STATION DIDN'T EVEN SCRATCH THE PAINT.

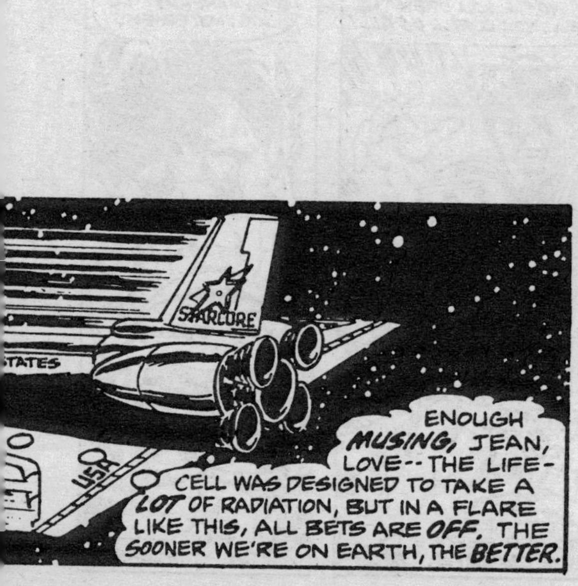
STARCORE
STATES
USA
ENOUGH MUSING, JEAN, LOVE--THE LIFE-CELL WAS DESIGNED TO TAKE A LOT OF RADIATION, BUT IN A FLARE LIKE THIS, ALL BETS ARE OFF. THE SOONER WE'RE ON EARTH, THE BETTER.

"ACCORDING TO *STAR-CORE*, THE FLARE'S A *MINUTE* AWAY-- AND IT'LL BE A *HALF-HOUR* AT LEAST BEFORE WE'RE *SAFE*.

"LORD, I'M SCARED...

"...I DON'T WANT TO *DIE*..."

SCOTT, *NO!* IF YOU OPEN THE LIFE-CELL, YOU'LL *KILL US ALL!*

LET ME *GO*, BLAST YOU!

LET ME *GO* TO HER BEFORE IT'S *TOO LATE.*

IT'S...*ALREADY* TOO LATE, MY FRIEND.

PLEASE, KURT--I *BEG* YOU...

...PLEASE...

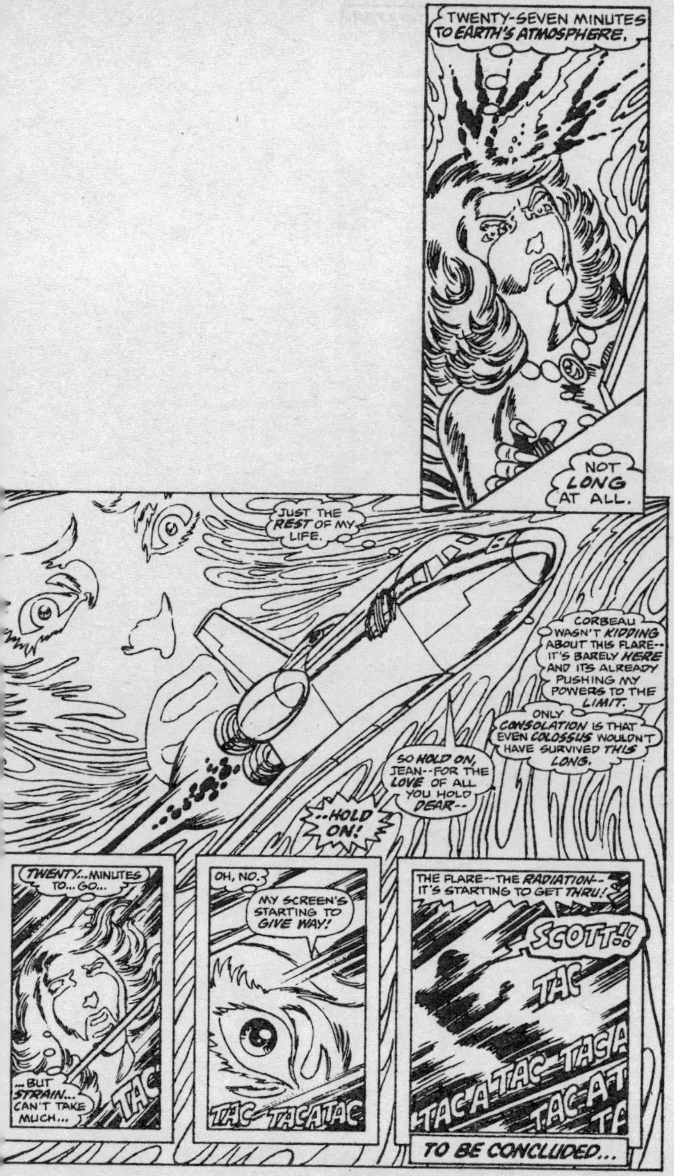

TWENTY-SEVEN MINUTES TO EARTH'S ATMOSPHERE.
NOT LONG AT ALL.
JUST THE REST OF MY LIFE.
CORBEAU WASN'T KIDDING ABOUT THIS FLARE-- IT'S BARELY HERE AND ITS ALREADY PUSHING MY POWERS TO THE LIMIT.
ONLY CONSOLATION IS THAT EVEN COLOSSUS WOULDN'T HAVE SURVIVED THIS LONG.
SO HOLD ON, JEAN--FOR THE LOVE OF ALL YOU HOLD DEAR--
--HOLD ON!
TWENTY...MINUTES TO...GO...
...BUT STRAIN... CAN'T TAKE MUCH...
TAC
OH, NO.
MY SCREEN'S STARTING TO GIVE WAY!
TAC TACATAC
THE FLARE--THE RADIATION-- IT'S STARTING TO GET THRU!
SCOTT!!
TAC
TAC-A-TAC-TAC-A
TAC-A-T
TA
TO BE CONCLUDED...

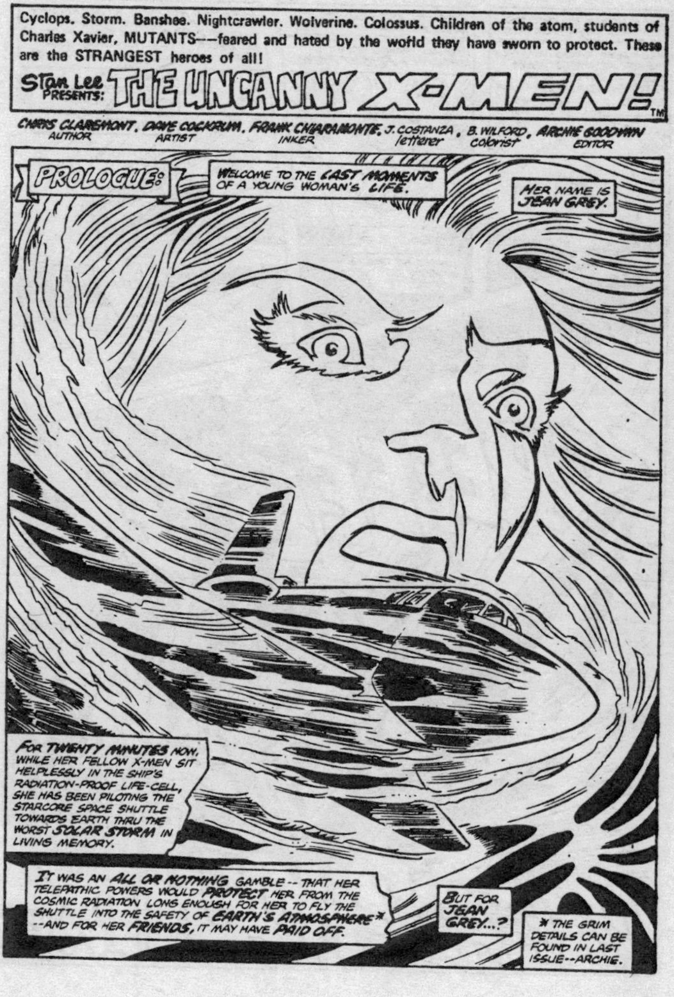
Cyclops. Storm. Banshee. Nightcrawler. Wolverine. Colossus. Children of the atom, students of Charles Xavier, MUTANTS—feared and hated by the world they have sworn to protect. These are the STRANGEST heroes of all!
Stan Lee PRESENTS: THE UNCANNY X-MEN! TM
CHRIS CLAREMONT, AUTHOR. DAVE COCKRUM, ARTIST. FRANK CHIARAMONTE, INKER. J. COSTANZA, letterer. B. WILFORD, colorist. ARCHIE GOODWIN, EDITOR
PROLOGUE:
WELCOME TO THE LAST MOMENTS OF A YOUNG WOMAN'S LIFE.
HER NAME IS JEAN GREY.
FOR TWENTY MINUTES NOW, WHILE HER FELLOW X-MEN SIT HELPLESSLY IN THE SHIP'S RADIATION-PROOF LIFE-CELL, SHE HAS BEEN PILOTING THE STARCORE SPACE SHUTTLE TOWARDS EARTH THRU THE WORST SOLAR STORM IN LIVING MEMORY.
IT WAS AN ALL OR NOTHING GAMBLE -- THAT HER TELEPATHIC POWERS WOULD PROTECT HER FROM THE COSMIC RADIATION LONG ENOUGH FOR HER TO FLY THE SHUTTLE INTO THE SAFETY OF EARTH'S ATMOSPHERE* --AND FOR HER FRIENDS, IT MAY HAVE PAID OFF.
BUT FOR JEAN GREY...?
* THE GRIM DETAILS CAN BE FOUND IN LAST ISSUE--ARCHIE.

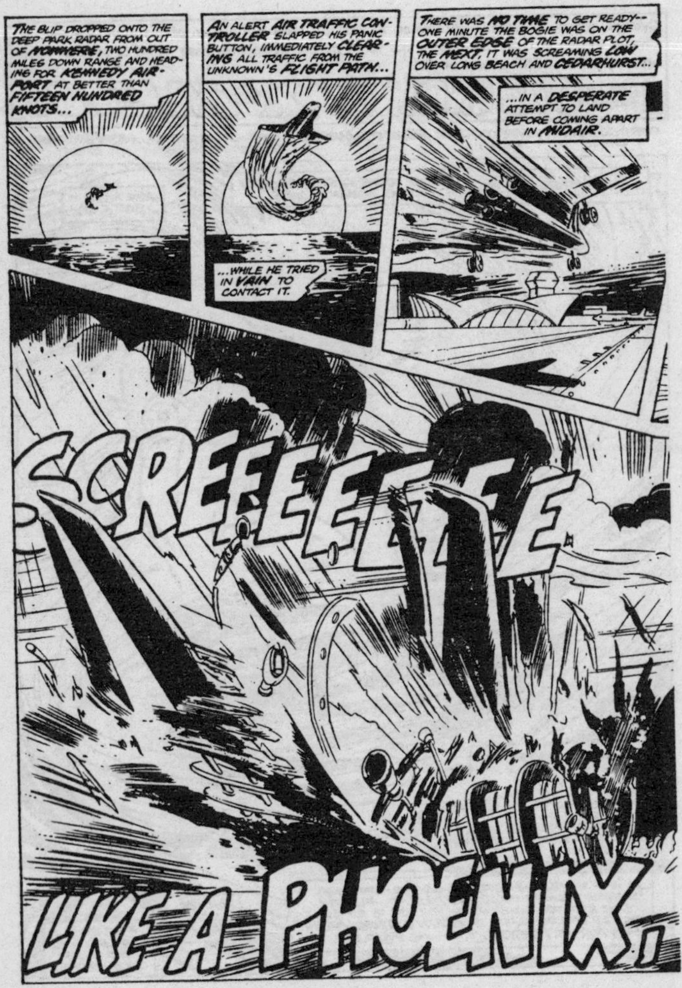
THE BLIP DROPPED ONTO THE DEEP PARK RADAR FROM OUT OF NOWHERE, TWO HUNDRED MILES DOWN RANGE AND HEADING FOR KENNEDY AIRPORT AT BETTER THAN FIFTEEN HUNDRED KNOTS...
AN ALERT AIR TRAFFIC CONTROLLER SLAPPED HIS PANIC BUTTON, IMMEDIATELY CLEARING ALL TRAFFIC FROM THE UNKNOWN'S FLIGHT PATH...
...WHILE HE TRIED IN VAIN TO CONTACT IT.
THERE WAS NO TIME TO GET READY-- ONE MINUTE THE BOGIE WAS ON THE OUTER EDGE OF THE RADAR PLOT, THE NEXT, IT WAS SCREAMING LOW OVER LONG BEACH AND CEDARHURST...
...IN A DESPERATE ATTEMPT TO LAND BEFORE COMING APART IN MIDAIR.
SCREEEEEE
LIKE A PHOENIX!

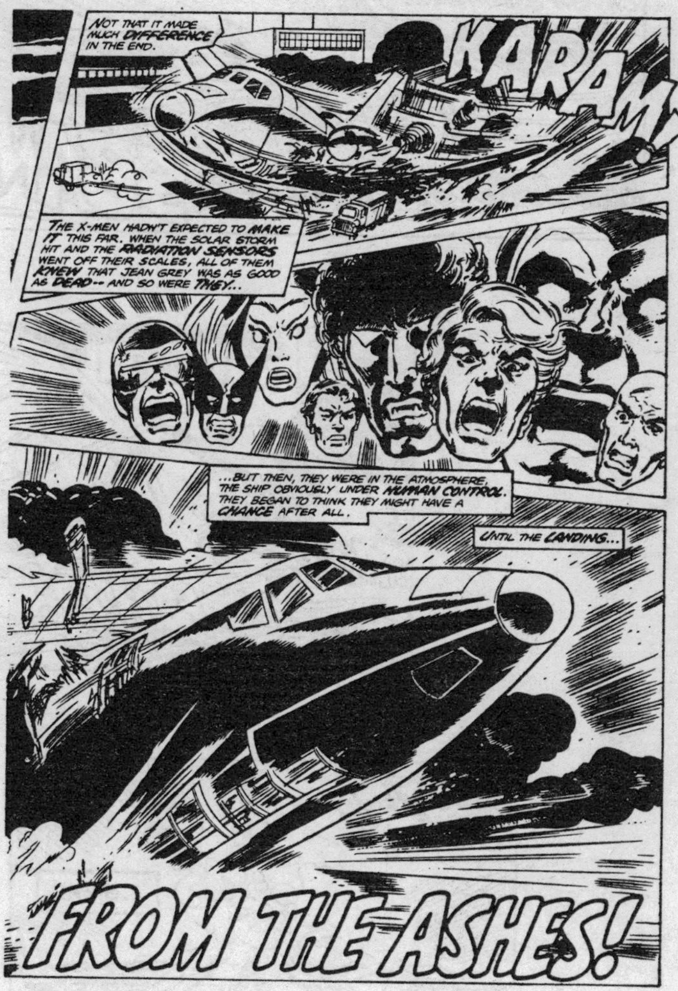
NOT THAT IT MADE MUCH DIFFERENCE IN THE END.
KARAM!
THE X-MEN HADN'T EXPECTED TO MAKE IT THIS FAR. WHEN THE SOLAR STORM HIT AND THE RADIATION SENSORS WENT OFF THEIR SCALES, ALL OF THEM KNEW THAT JEAN GREY WAS AS GOOD AS DEAD-- AND SO WERE THEY...
...BUT THEN, THEY WERE IN THE ATMOSPHERE, THE SHIP OBVIOUSLY UNDER HUMAN CONTROL. THEY BEGAN TO THINK THEY MIGHT HAVE A CHANCE AFTER ALL.
UNTIL THE LANDING...
FROM THE ASHES!

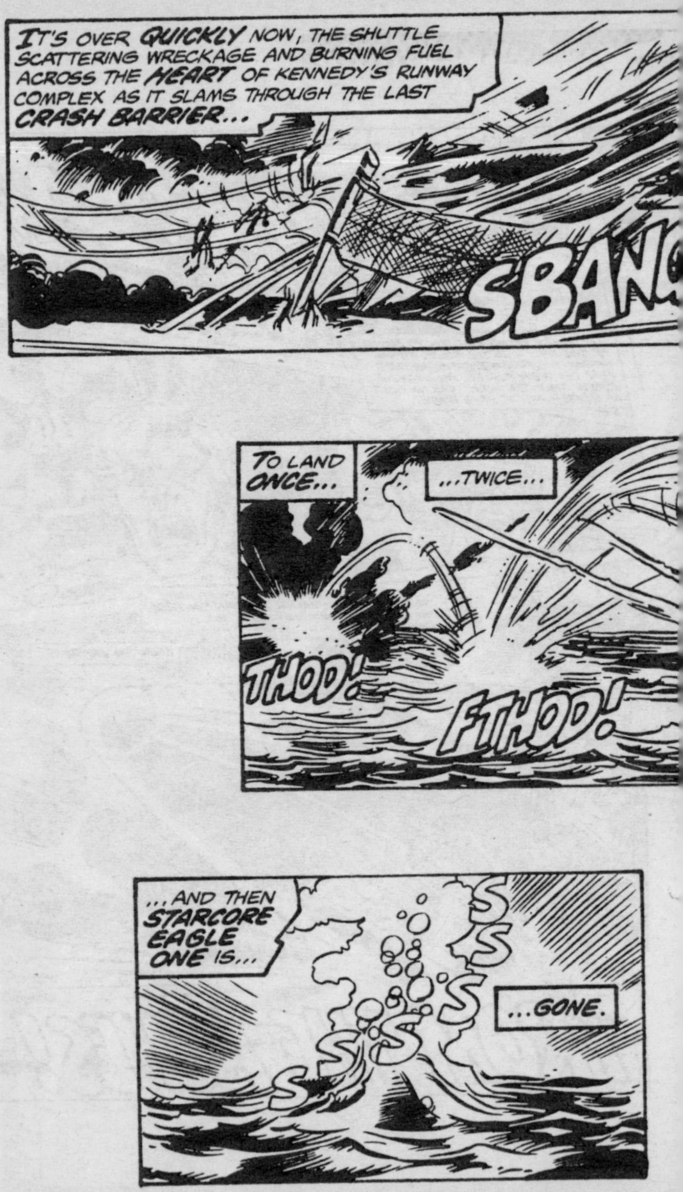
IT'S OVER QUICKLY NOW, THE SHUTTLE SCATTERING WRECKAGE AND BURNING FUEL ACROSS THE HEART OF KENNEDY'S RUNWAY COMPLEX AS IT SLAMS THROUGH THE LAST CRASH BARRIER...
SBANG
TO LAND ONCE...
...TWICE...
THOD!
FTHOD!
...AND THEN STARCORE EAGLE ONE IS...
SSSSSS
...GONE.

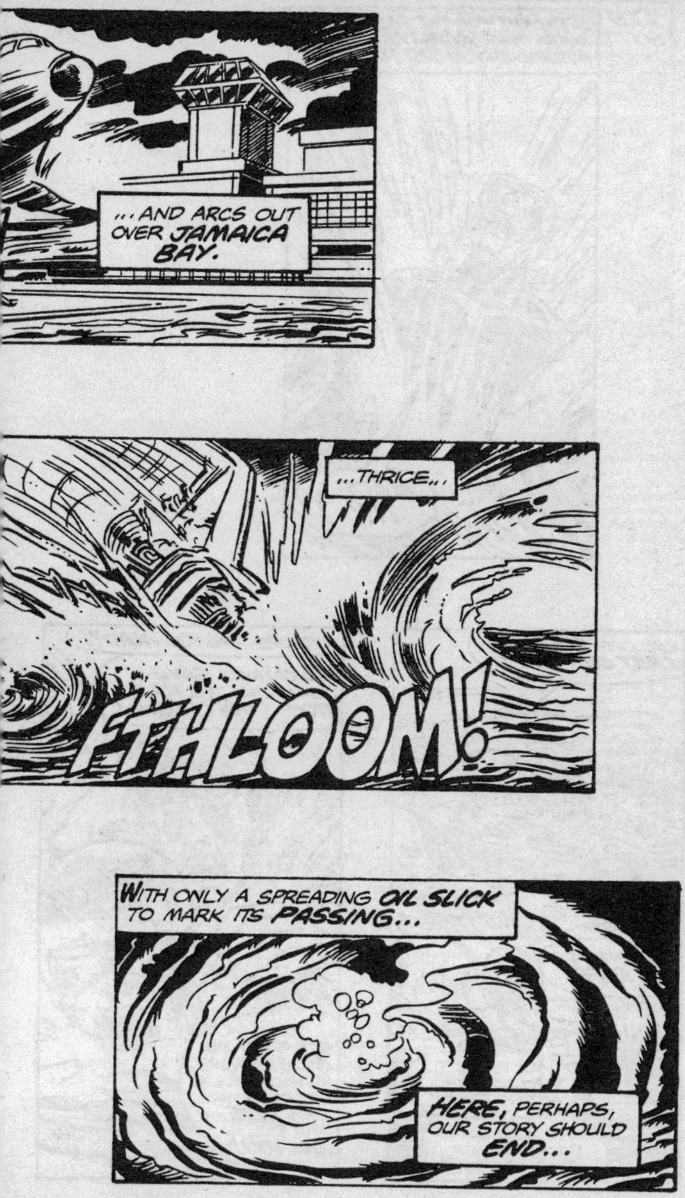
...AND ARCS OUT OVER JAMAICA BAY.
...THRICE...
FTHLOOM!
WITH ONLY A SPREADING OIL SLICK TO MARK ITS PASSING...
HERE, PERHAPS, OUR STORY SHOULD END...

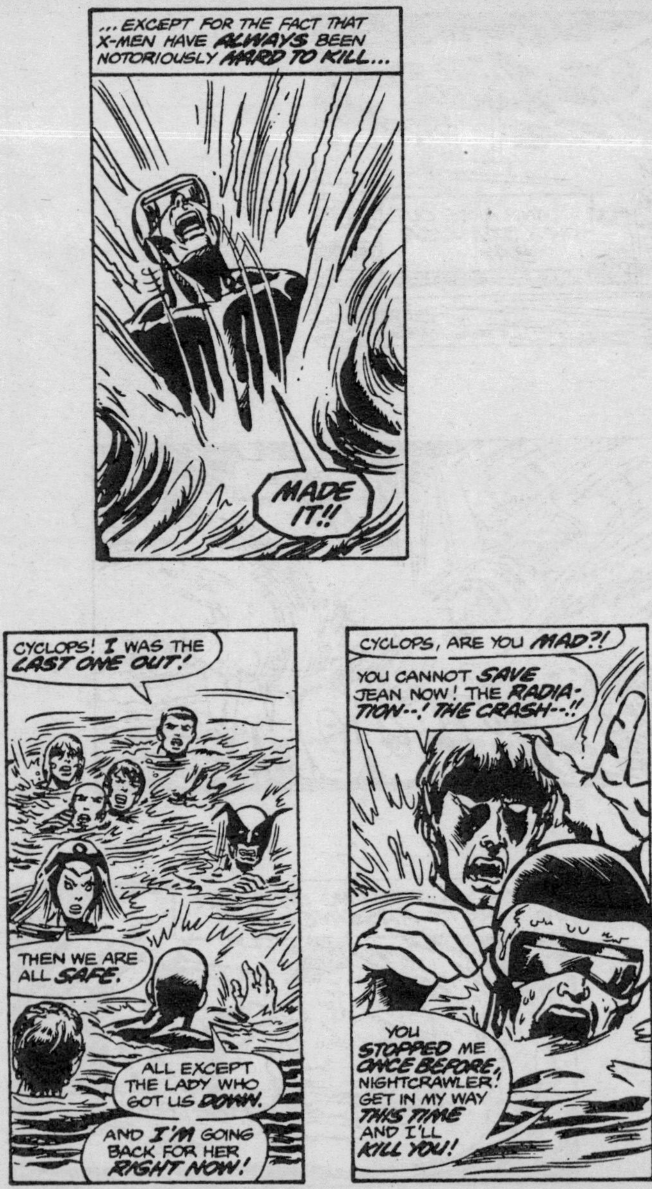
...EXCEPT FOR THE FACT THAT X-MEN HAVE ALWAYS BEEN NOTORIOUSLY HARD TO KILL...
MADE IT!!
CYCLOPS! I WAS THE LAST ONE OUT!
THEN WE ARE ALL SAFE.
ALL EXCEPT THE LADY WHO GOT US DOWN.
AND I'M GOING BACK FOR HER RIGHT NOW!
CYCLOPS, ARE YOU MAD?!
YOU CANNOT SAVE JEAN NOW! THE RADIATION--! THE CRASH--!!
YOU STOPPED ME ONCE BEFORE, NIGHTCRAWLER! GET IN MY WAY THIS TIME AND I'LL KILL YOU!

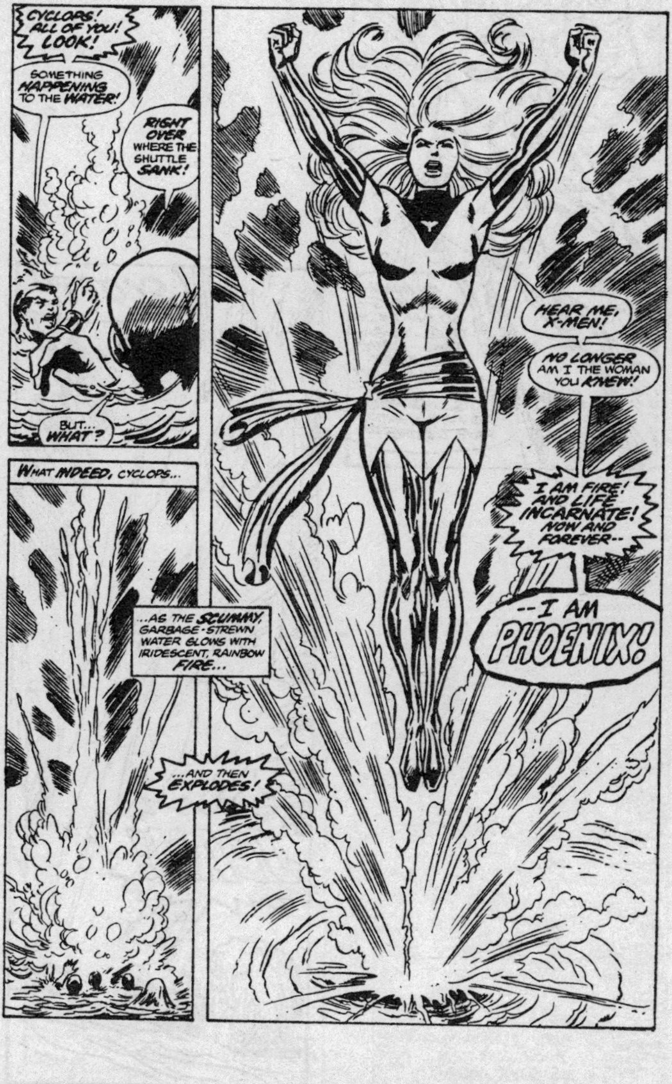

CYCLOPS! ALL OF YOU! LOOK!
SOMETHING HAPPENING TO THE WATER!
RIGHT OVER WHERE THE SHUTTLE SANK!
BUT... WHAT?
WHAT INDEED, CYCLOPS...
...AS THE SCUMMY, GARBAGE-STREWN WATER GLOWS WITH IRIDESCENT, RAINBOW FIRE...
...AND THEN EXPLODES!
HEAR ME, X-MEN!
NO LONGER AM I THE WOMAN YOU KNEW!
I AM FIRE! AND LIFE INCARNATE! NOW AND FOREVER--
--I AM PHOENIX!

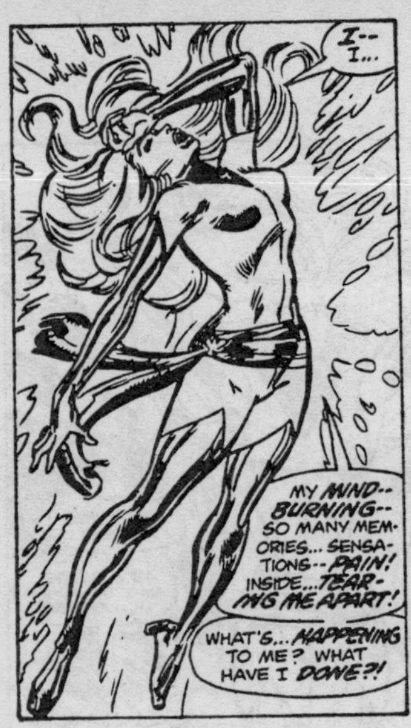
I-- I...
MY MIND-- BURNING-- SO MANY MEMORIES... SENSATIONS-- PAIN! INSIDE... TEARING ME APART!
WHAT'S... HAPPENING TO ME? WHAT HAVE I DONE?!

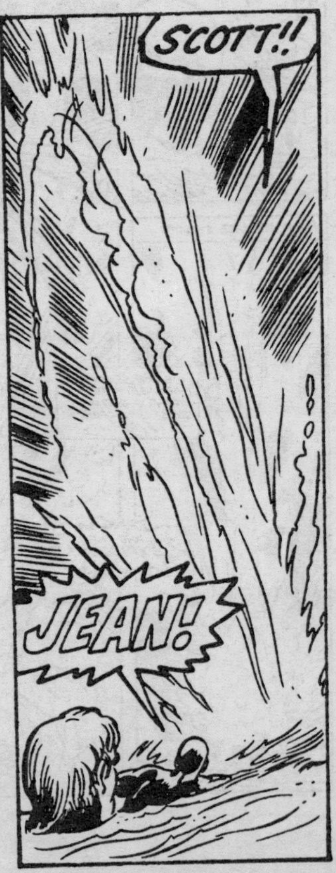
SCOTT!!
JEAN!

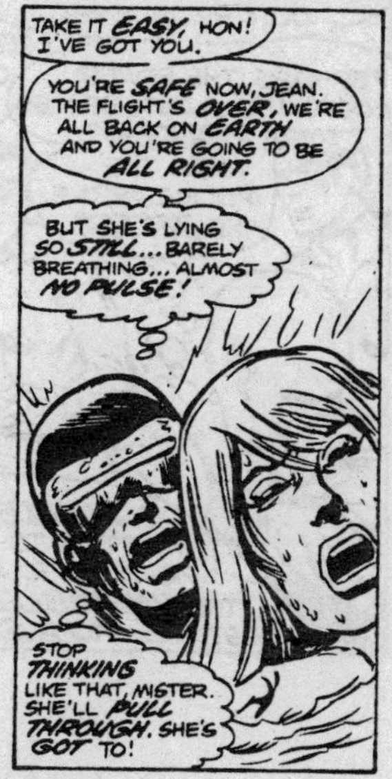
TAKE IT EASY, HON! I'VE GOT YOU.
YOU'RE SAFE NOW, JEAN. THE FLIGHT'S OVER, WE'RE ALL BACK ON EARTH AND YOU'RE GOING TO BE ALL RIGHT.
BUT SHE'S LYING SO STILL... BARELY BREATHING... ALMOST NO PULSE!
STOP THINKING LIKE THAT, MISTER. SHE'LL PULL THROUGH. SHE'S GOT TO!

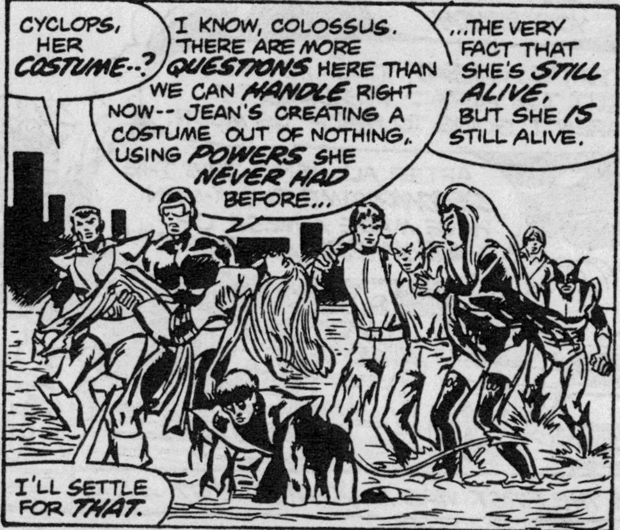
CYCLOPS, HER COSTUME--?
I KNOW, COLOSSUS. THERE ARE MORE QUESTIONS HERE THAN WE CAN HANDLE RIGHT NOW-- JEAN'S CREATING A COSTUME OUT OF NOTHING, USING POWERS SHE NEVER HAD BEFORE...
...THE VERY FACT THAT SHE'S STILL ALIVE, BUT SHE IS STILL ALIVE.
I'LL SETTLE FOR THAT.

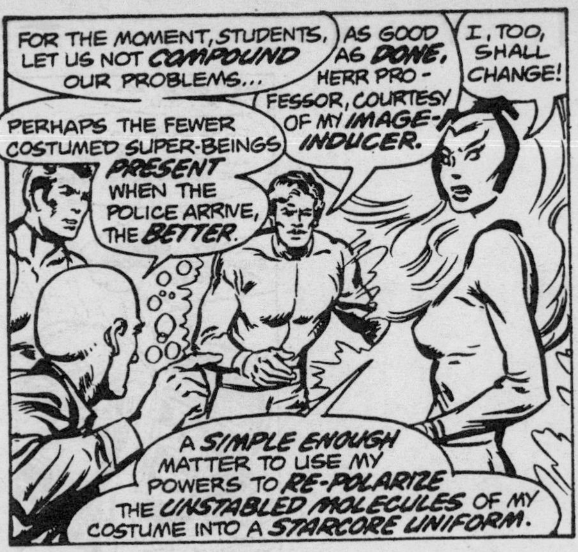
FOR THE MOMENT, STUDENTS, LET US NOT COMPOUND OUR PROBLEMS...
PERHAPS THE FEWER COSTUMED SUPER-BEINGS PRESENT WHEN THE POLICE ARRIVE, THE BETTER.
AS GOOD AS DONE, HERR PRO-FESSOR, COURTESY OF MY IMAGE-INDUCER.
I, TOO, SHALL CHANGE!
A SIMPLE ENOUGH MATTER TO USE MY POWERS TO RE-POLARIZE THE UNSTABLED MOLECULES OF MY COSTUME INTO A STARCORE UNIFORM.

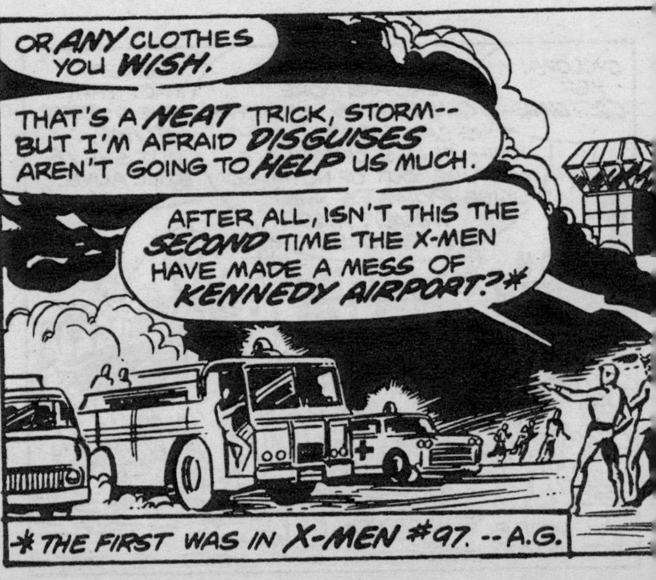
OR ANY CLOTHES YOU WISH.
THAT'S A NEAT TRICK, STORM--BUT I'M AFRAID DISGUISES AREN'T GOING TO HELP US MUCH.
AFTER ALL, ISN'T THIS THE SECOND TIME THE X-MEN HAVE MADE A MESS OF KENNEDY AIRPORT?*
*THE FIRST WAS IN X-MEN #97. --A.G.

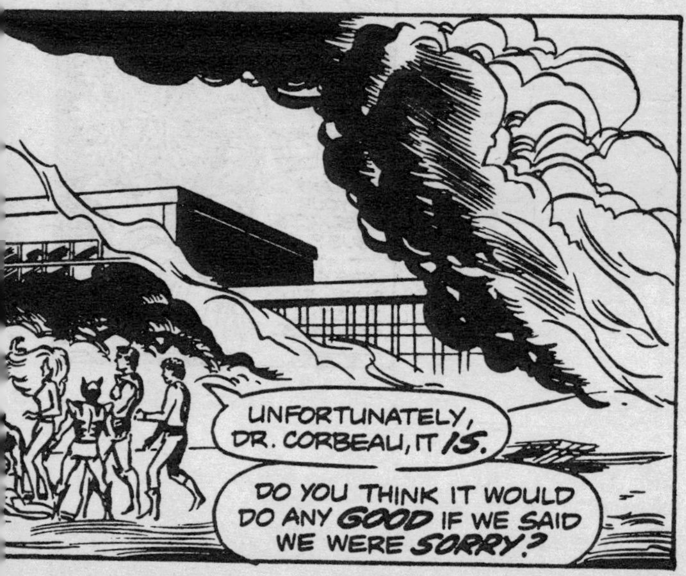
UNFORTUNATELY, DR. CORBEAU, IT IS.
DO YOU THINK IT WOULD DO ANY GOOD IF WE SAID WE WERE SORRY?

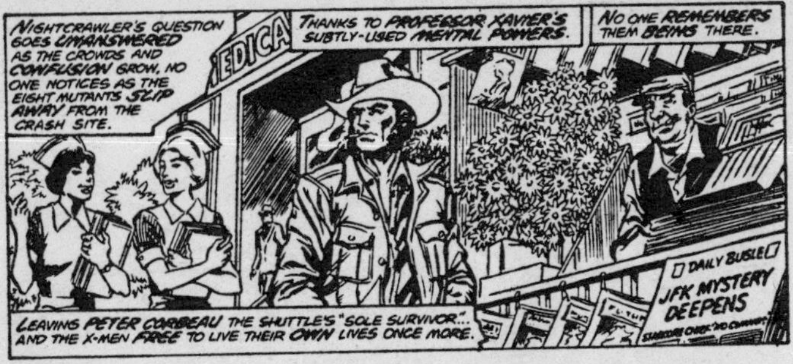
NIGHTCRAWLER'S QUESTION GOES UNANSWERED AS THE CROWDS AND CONFUSION GROW. NO ONE NOTICES AS THE EIGHT MUTANTS SLIP AWAY FROM THE CRASH SITE.
EDICA
THANKS TO PROFESSOR XAVIER'S SUBTLY-USED MENTAL POWERS.
NO ONE REMEMBERS THEM BEING THERE.
DAILY BUGLE
JFK MYSTERY DEEPENS
LEAVING PETER CORBEAU THE SHUTTLE'S "SOLE SURVIVOR"... AND THE X-MEN FREE TO LIVE THEIR OWN LIVES ONCE MORE.

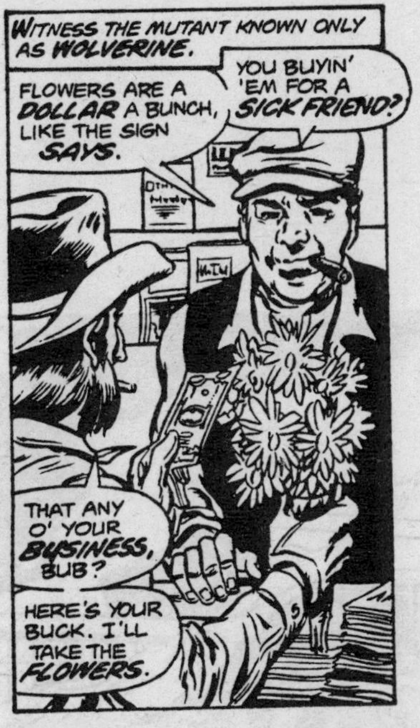
WITNESS THE MUTANT KNOWN ONLY AS WOLVERINE.
FLOWERS ARE A DOLLAR A BUNCH, LIKE THE SIGN SAYS.
YOU BUYIN' 'EM FOR A SICK FRIEND?
THAT ANY O' YOUR BUSINESS, BUB?
HERE'S YOUR BUCK. I'LL TAKE THE FLOWERS.

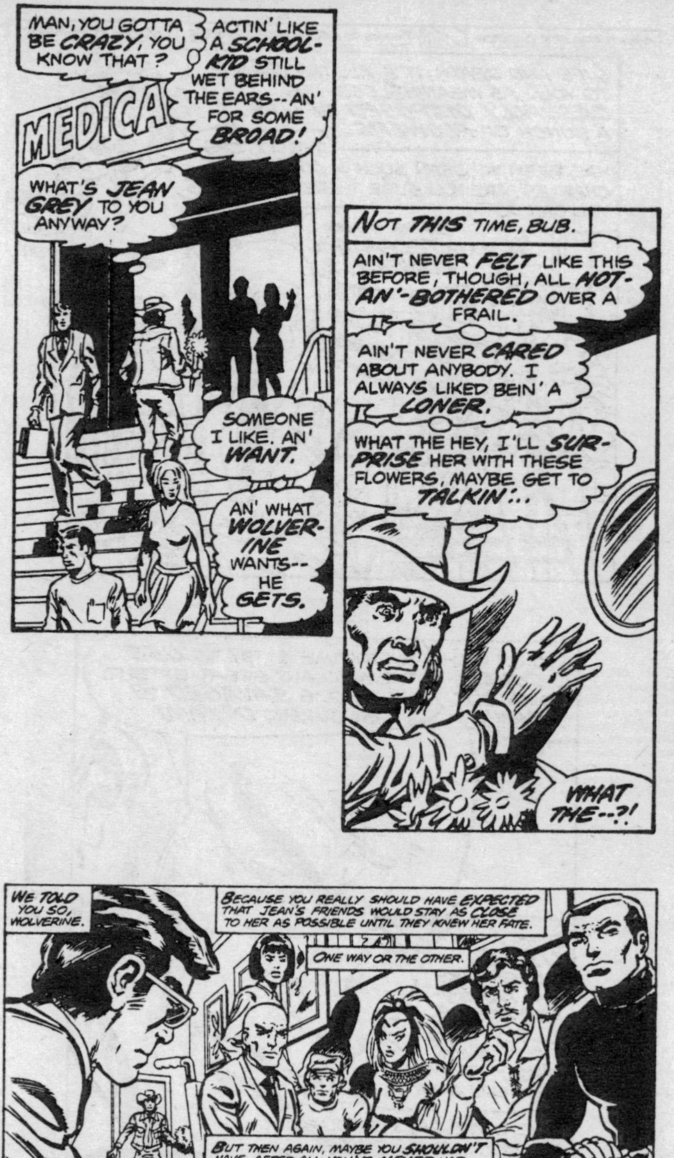
MAN, YOU GOTTA BE CRAZY, YOU KNOW THAT?
ACTIN' LIKE A SCHOOL-KID STILL WET BEHIND THE EARS-- AN' FOR SOME BROAD!
MEDICA
WHAT'S JEAN GREY TO YOU ANYWAY?
SOMEONE I LIKE. AN' WANT.
AN' WHAT WOLVER-INE WANTS-- HE GETS.
NOT THIS TIME, BUB.
AIN'T NEVER FELT LIKE THIS BEFORE, THOUGH, ALL NOT-AN'-BOTHERED OVER A FRAIL.
AIN'T NEVER CARED ABOUT ANYBODY. I ALWAYS LIKED BEIN' A LONER.
WHAT THE HEY, I'LL SUR-PRISE HER WITH THESE FLOWERS, MAYBE GET TO TALKIN'...
WHAT THE--?!
WE TOLD YOU SO, WOLVERINE.
BECAUSE YOU REALLY SHOULD HAVE EXPECTED THAT JEAN'S FRIENDS WOULD STAY AS CLOSE TO HER AS POSSIBLE UNTIL THEY KNEW HER FATE.
ONE WAY OR THE OTHER.
BUT THEN AGAIN, MAYBE YOU SHOULDN'T HAVE. AFTER ALL, YOU'VE NEVER HAD ANY FRIENDS.

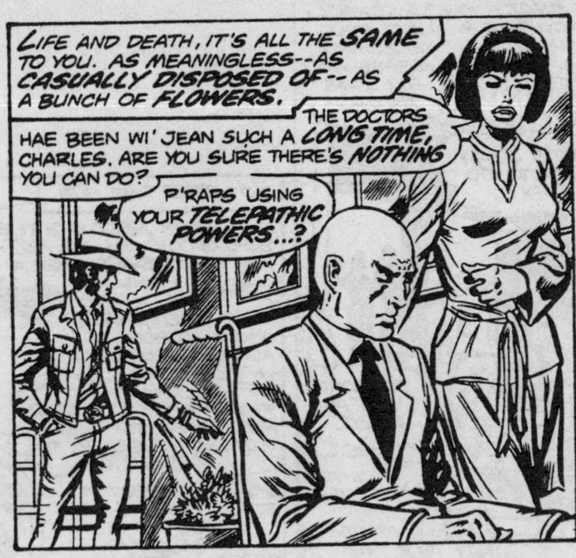
LIFE AND DEATH, IT'S ALL THE SAME TO YOU. AS MEANINGLESS--AS CASUALLY DISPOSED OF--AS A BUNCH OF FLOWERS.
THE DOCTORS HAE BEEN WI' JEAN SUCH A LONG TIME, CHARLES. ARE YOU SURE THERE'S NOTHING YOU CAN DO?
P'RAPS USING YOUR TELEPATHIC POWERS...?

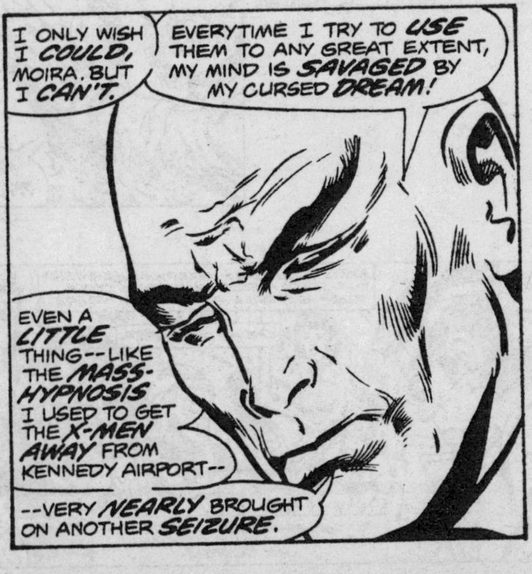
I ONLY WISH I COULD, MOIRA. BUT I CAN'T.
EVERYTIME I TRY TO USE THEM TO ANY GREAT EXTENT, MY MIND IS SAVAGED BY MY CURSED DREAM!
EVEN A LITTLE THING--LIKE THE MASS-HYPNOSIS I USED TO GET THE X-MEN AWAY FROM KENNEDY AIRPORT--
--VERY NEARLY BROUGHT ON ANOTHER SEIZURE.

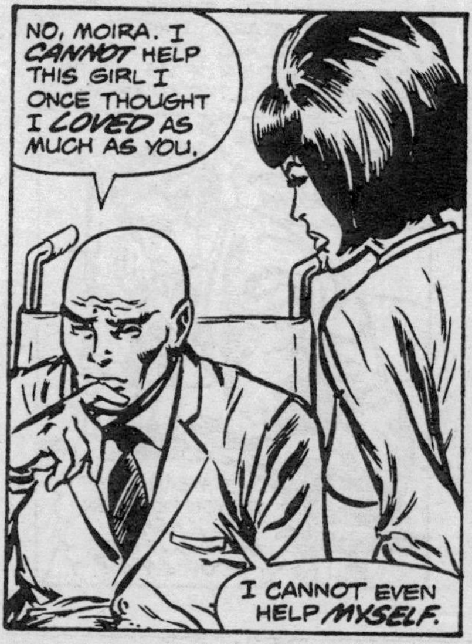
NO, MOIRA. I CANNOT HELP THIS GIRL I ONCE THOUGHT I LOVED AS MUCH AS YOU.
I CANNOT EVEN HELP MYSELF.

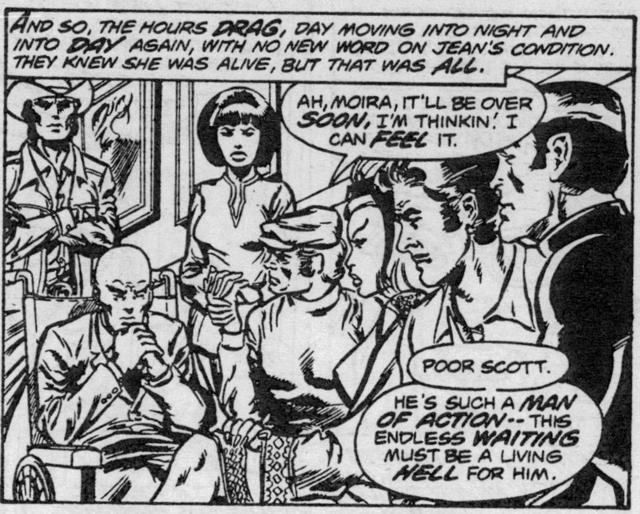
AND SO, THE HOURS DRAG, DAY MOVING INTO NIGHT AND INTO DAY AGAIN, WITH NO NEW WORD ON JEAN'S CONDITION. THEY KNEW SHE WAS ALIVE, BUT THAT WAS ALL.
AH, MOIRA, IT'LL BE OVER SOON, I'M THINKIN'. I CAN FEEL IT.
POOR SCOTT.
HE'S SUCH A MAN OF ACTION-- THIS ENDLESS WAITING MUST BE A LIVING HELL FOR HIM.

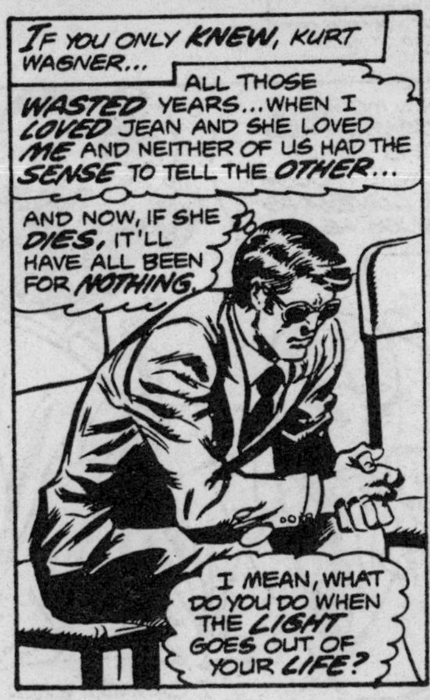
IF YOU ONLY KNEW, KURT WAGNER...
ALL THOSE WASTED YEARS...WHEN I LOVED JEAN AND SHE LOVED ME AND NEITHER OF US HAD THE SENSE TO TELL THE OTHER...
AND NOW, IF SHE DIES, IT'LL HAVE ALL BEEN FOR NOTHING.
I MEAN, WHAT DO YOU DO WHEN THE LIGHT GOES OUT OF YOUR LIFE?

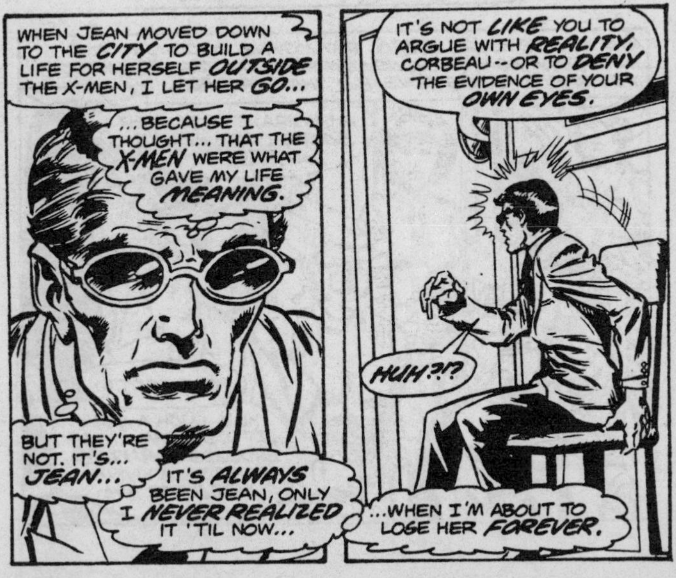
WHEN JEAN MOVED DOWN TO THE CITY TO BUILD A LIFE FOR HERSELF OUTSIDE THE X-MEN, I LET HER GO...
...BECAUSE I THOUGHT... THAT THE X-MEN WERE WHAT GAVE MY LIFE MEANING.
BUT THEY'RE NOT. IT'S... JEAN...
IT'S ALWAYS BEEN JEAN, ONLY I NEVER REALIZED IT 'TIL NOW...
IT'S NOT LIKE YOU TO ARGUE WITH REALITY, CORBEAU--OR TO DENY THE EVIDENCE OF YOUR OWN EYES.
HUH?!?
...WHEN I'M ABOUT TO LOSE HER FOREVER.

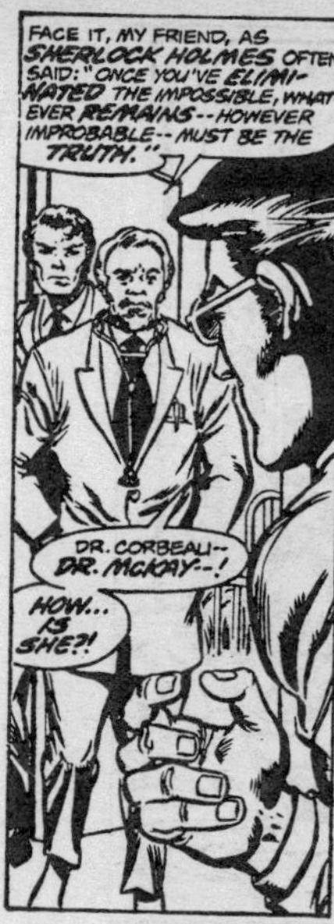
FACE IT, MY FRIEND, AS SHERLOCK HOLMES OFTEN SAID: "ONCE YOU'VE ELIMINATED THE IMPOSSIBLE, WHATEVER REMAINS--HOWEVER IMPROBABLE-- MUST BE THE TRUTH."
DR. CORBEAU-- DR. McKAY--!
HOW... IS SHE?!

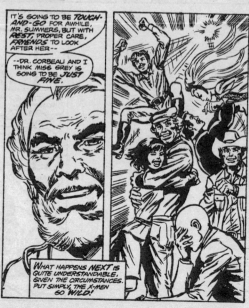

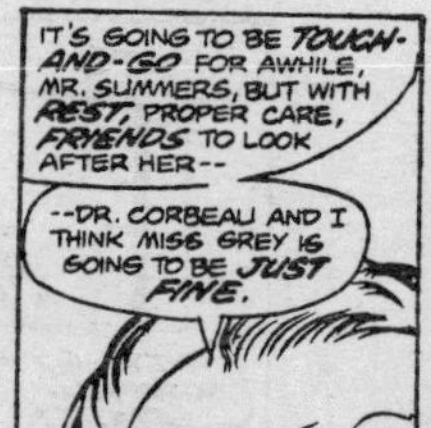
IT'S GOING TO BE TOUCH-AND-GO FOR AWHILE, MR. SUMMERS, BUT WITH REST, PROPER CARE, FRIENDS TO LOOK AFTER HER--
--DR. CORBEAU AND I THINK MISS GREY IS GOING TO BE JUST FINE.

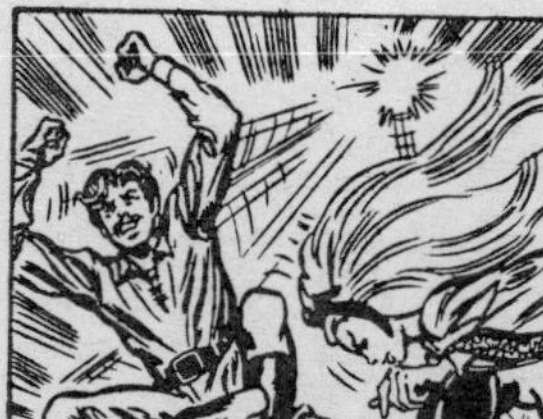
WHAT HAPPENS NEXT IS QUITE UNDERSTANDABLE, GIVEN THE CIRCUMSTANCES. PUT SIMPLY, THE X-MEN GO WILD!

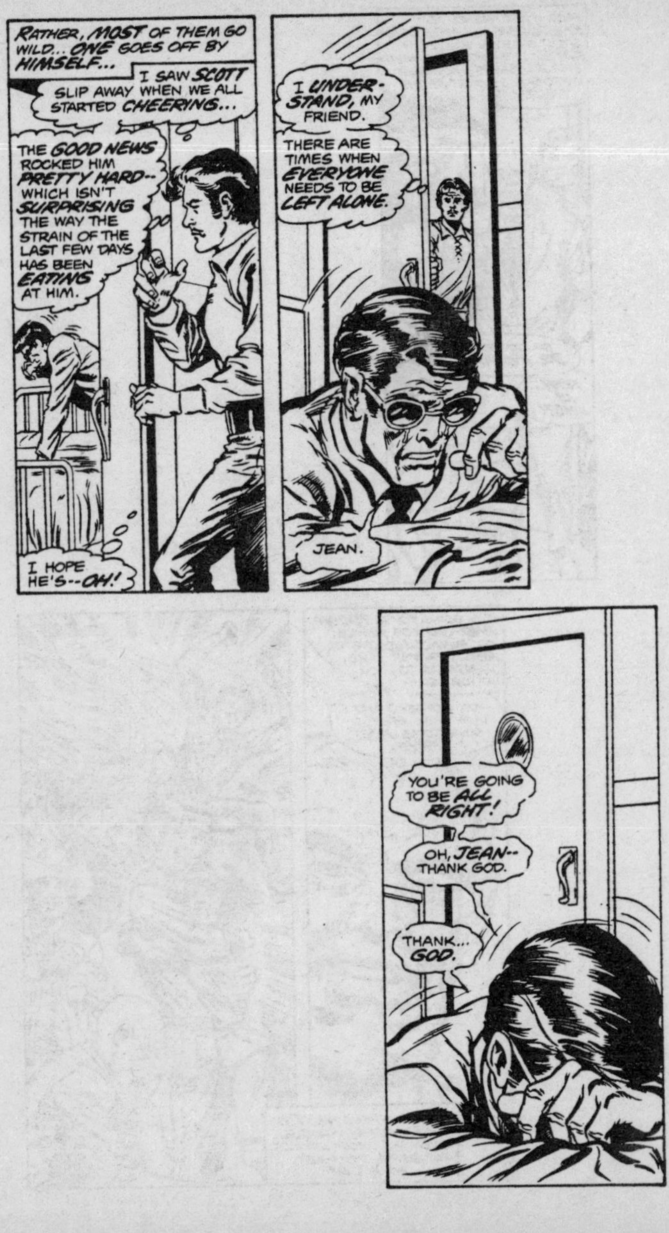
RATHER, MOST OF THEM GO WILD... ONE GOES OFF BY HIMSELF...
I SAW SCOTT SLIP AWAY WHEN WE ALL STARTED CHEERING...
THE GOOD NEWS ROCKED HIM PRETTY HARD-- WHICH ISN'T SURPRISING THE WAY THE STRAIN OF THE LAST FEW DAYS HAS BEEN EATING AT HIM.
I HOPE HE'S--OH!
I UNDERSTAND, MY FRIEND.
THERE ARE TIMES WHEN EVERYONE NEEDS TO BE LEFT ALONE.
JEAN.
YOU'RE GOING TO BE ALL RIGHT!
OH, JEAN-- THANK GOD.
THANK... GOD.

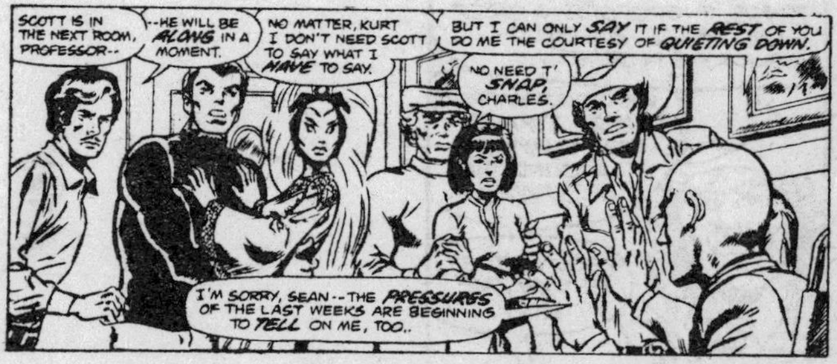
SCOTT IS IN THE NEXT ROOM, PROFESSOR--
--HE WILL BE ALONG IN A MOMENT.
NO MATTER, KURT I DON'T NEED SCOTT TO SAY WHAT I HAVE TO SAY.
BUT I CAN ONLY SAY IT IF THE REST OF YOU DO ME THE COURTESY OF QUIETING DOWN.
NO NEED T' SNAP, CHARLES.
I'M SORRY, SEAN--THE PRESSURES OF THE LAST WEEKS ARE BEGINNING TO TELL ON ME, TOO..

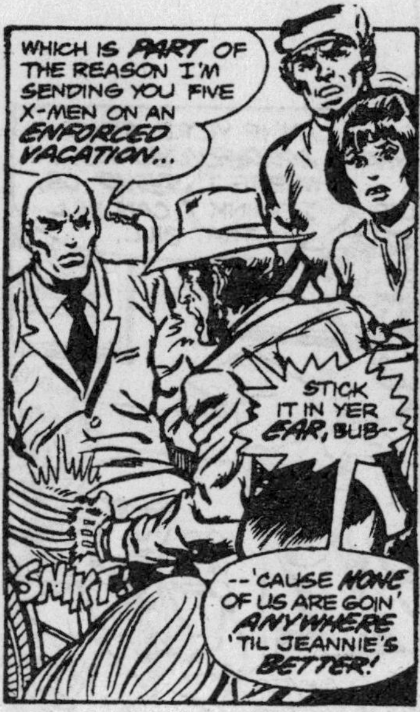
WHICH IS PART OF THE REASON I'M SENDING YOU FIVE X-MEN ON AN ENFORCED VACATION...
STICK IT IN YER EAR, BUB--
SNIKT!
--'CAUSE NONE OF US ARE GOIN' ANYWHERE 'TIL JEANNIE'S BETTER!

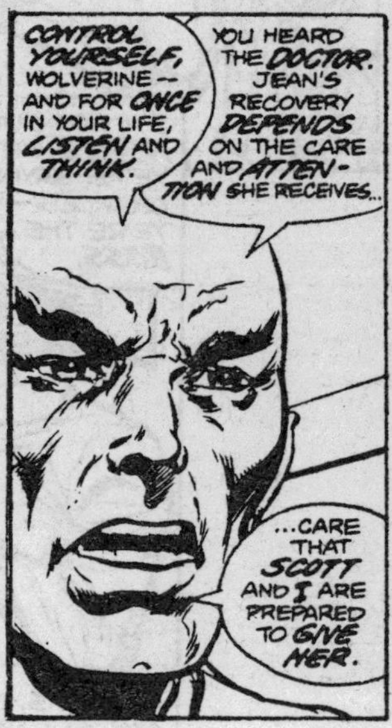
CONTROL YOURSELF, WOLVERINE--AND FOR ONCE IN YOUR LIFE, LISTEN AND THINK.
YOU HEARD THE DOCTOR. JEAN'S RECOVERY DEPENDS ON THE CARE AND ATTENTION SHE RECEIVES...
...CARE THAT SCOTT AND I ARE PREPARED TO GIVE HER.

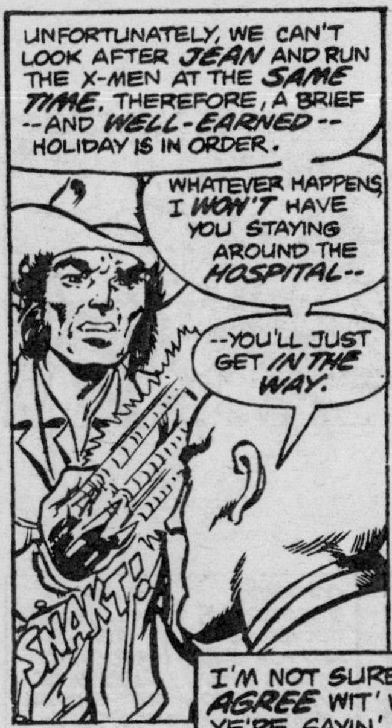
UNFORTUNATELY, WE CAN'T LOOK AFTER JEAN AND RUN THE X-MEN AT THE SAME TIME. THEREFORE, A BRIEF --AND WELL-EARNED-- HOLIDAY IS IN ORDER.
WHATEVER HAPPENS, I WON'T HAVE YOU STAYING AROUND THE HOSPITAL--
--YOU'LL JUST GET IN THE WAY.
SNAKT!

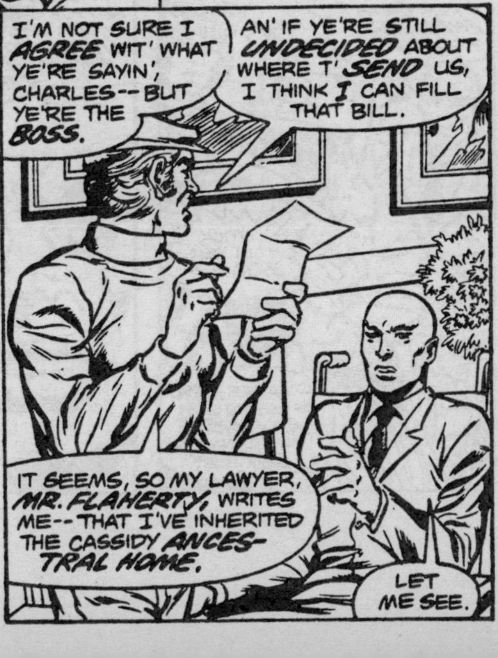
I'M NOT SURE I AGREE WIT' WHAT YE'RE SAYIN', CHARLES--BUT YE'RE THE BOSS.
AN' IF YE'RE STILL UNDECIDED ABOUT WHERE T' SEND US, I THINK I CAN FILL THAT BILL.
IT SEEMS, SO MY LAWYER, MR. FLAHERTY, WRITES ME--THAT I'VE INHERITED THE CASSIDY ANCES-TRAL HOME.
LET ME SEE.

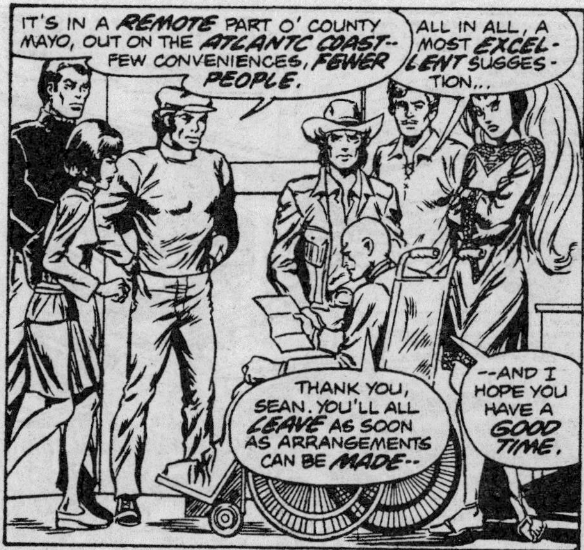
IT'S IN A REMOTE PART O' COUNTY MAYO, OUT ON THE ATLANTC COAST-- FEW CONVENIENCES, FEWER PEOPLE.
ALL IN ALL, A MOST EXCEL-LENT SUGGES-TION...
THANK YOU, SEAN. YOU'LL ALL LEAVE AS SOON AS ARRANGEMENTS CAN BE MADE--
--AND I HOPE YOU HAVE A GOOD TIME.

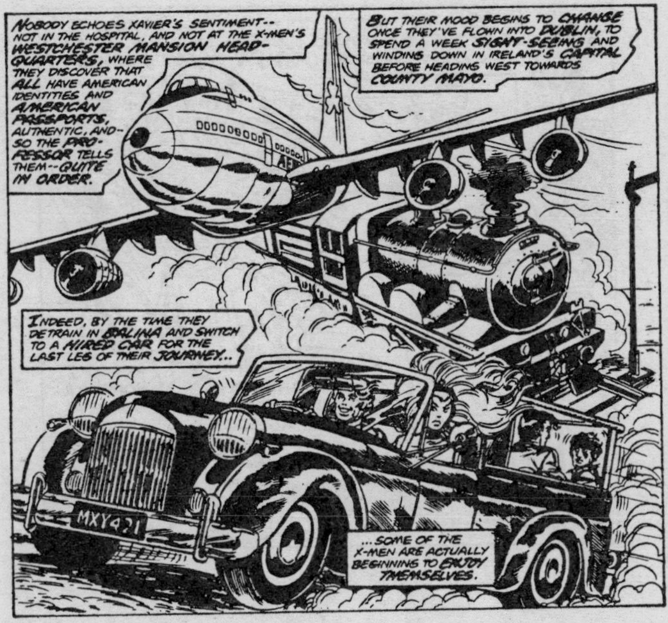
NOBODY ECHOES XAVIER'S SENTIMENT-- NOT IN THE HOSPITAL, AND NOT AT THE X-MEN'S WESTCHESTER MANSION HEAD-QUARTERS, WHERE THEY DISCOVER THAT ALL HAVE AMERICAN IDENTITIES AND AMERICAN PASSPORTS, AUTHENTIC, AND--SO THE PRO-FESSOR TELLS THEM--QUITE IN ORDER.
BUT THEIR MOOD BEGINS TO CHANGE ONCE THEY'VE FLOWN INTO DUBLIN, TO SPEND A WEEK SIGHT-SEEING AND WINDING DOWN IN IRELAND'S CAPITAL BEFORE HEADING WEST TOWARDS COUNTY MAYO.
INDEED, BY THE TIME THEY DETRAIN IN BALINA AND SWITCH TO A HIRED CAR FOR THE LAST LEG OF THEIR JOURNEY...
...SOME OF THE X-MEN ARE ACTUALLY BEGINNING TO ENJOY THEMSELVES.

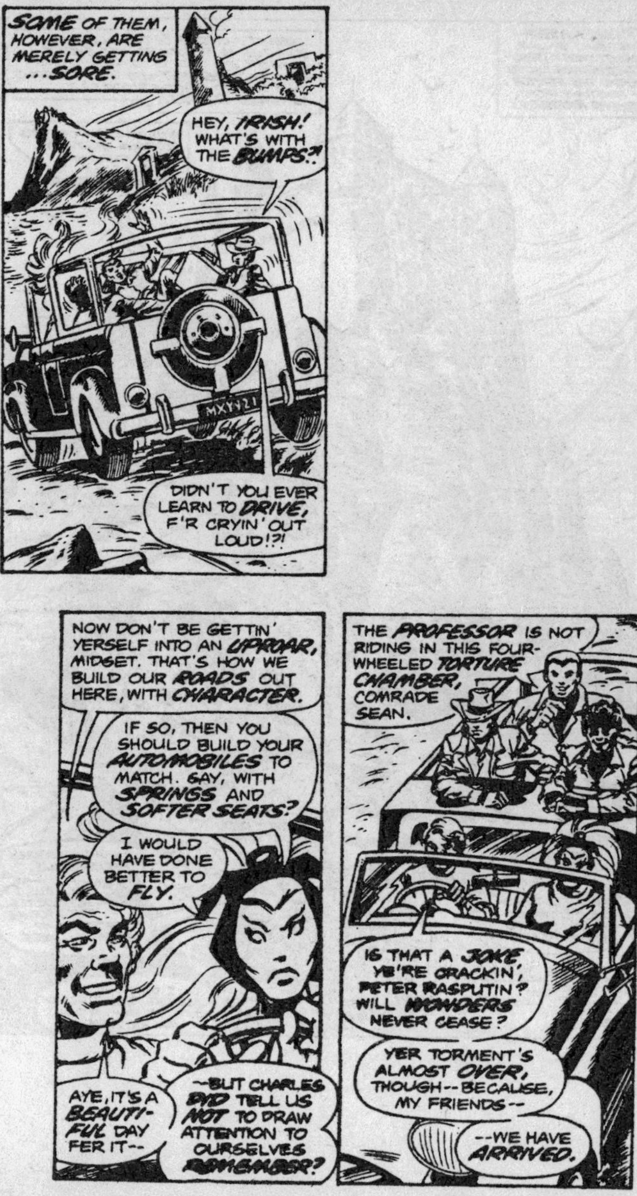
SOME OF THEM, HOWEVER, ARE MERELY GETTING ...SORE.
HEY, IRISH! WHAT'S WITH THE BUMPS?!
MXY 121
DIDN'T YOU EVER LEARN TO DRIVE, F'R CRYIN' OUT LOUD!?!
NOW DON'T BE GETTIN' YERSELF INTO AN UPROAR, MIDGET. THAT'S HOW WE BUILD OUR ROADS OUT HERE, WITH CHARACTER.
IF SO, THEN YOU SHOULD BUILD YOUR AUTOMOBILES TO MATCH. SAY, WITH SPRINGS AND SOFTER SEATS?
I WOULD HAVE DONE BETTER TO FLY.
AYE, IT'S A BEAUTI-FUL DAY FER IT--
--BUT CHARLES DID TELL US NOT TO DRAW ATTENTION TO OURSELVES REMEMBER?
THE PROFESSOR IS NOT RIDING IN THIS FOUR-WHEELED TORTURE CHAMBER, COMRADE SEAN.
IS THAT A JOKE YE'RE CRACKIN', PETER RASPUTIN? WILL WONDERS NEVER CEASE?
YER TORMENT'S ALMOST OVER, THOUGH--BECAUSE, MY FRIENDS--
--WE HAVE ARRIVED.

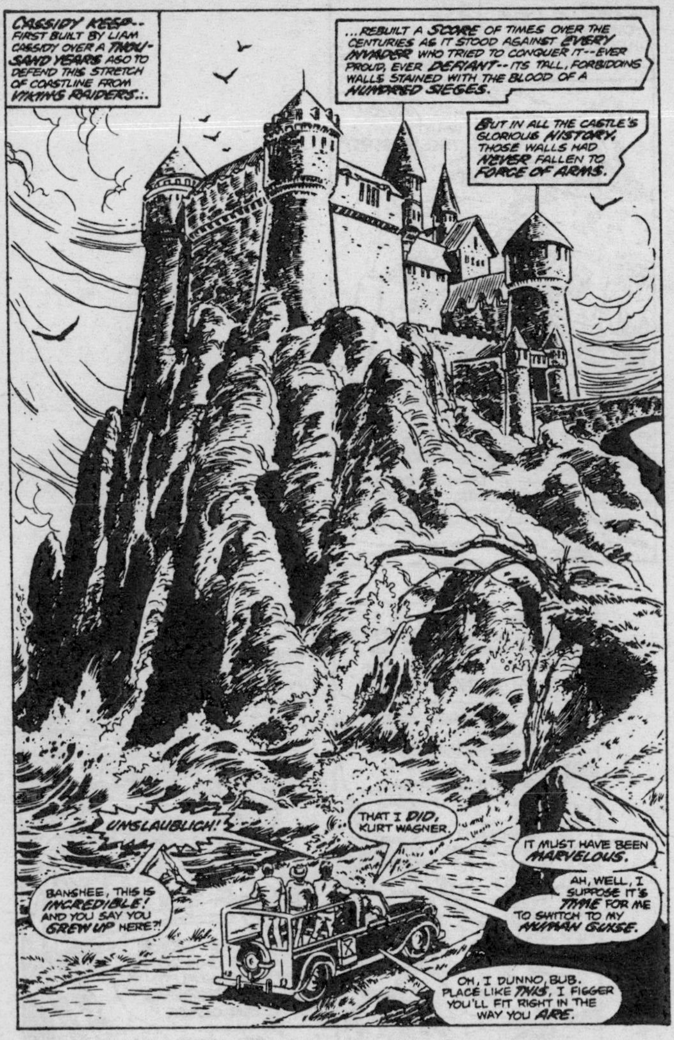
CASSIDY KEEP-- FIRST BUILT BY LIAM CASSIDY OVER A THOUSAND YEARS AGO TO DEFEND THIS STRETCH OF COASTLINE FROM VIKING RAIDERS...
...REBUILT A SCORE OF TIMES OVER THE CENTURIES AS IT STOOD AGAINST EVERY INVADER WHO TRIED TO CONQUER IT--EVER PROUD, EVER DEFIANT-- ITS TALL, FORBIDDING WALLS STAINED WITH THE BLOOD OF A HUNDRED SIEGES.
BUT IN ALL THE CASTLE'S GLORIOUS HISTORY, THOSE WALLS HAD NEVER FALLEN TO FORCE OF ARMS.
UNGLAUBLICH!
BANSHEE, THIS IS INCREDIBLE! AND YOU SAY YOU GREW UP HERE?!
THAT I DID, KURT WAGNER.
IT MUST HAVE BEEN MARVELOUS.
AH, WELL, I SUPPOSE IT'S TIME FOR ME TO SWITCH TO MY HUMAN GUISE.
OH, I DUNNO, BUB. PLACE LIKE THIS, I FIGGER YOU'LL FIT RIGHT IN THE WAY YOU ARE.

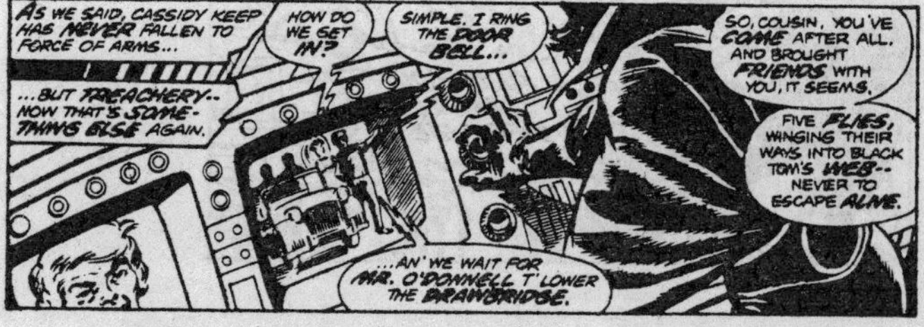
AS WE SAID, CASSIDY KEEP HAS NEVER FALLEN TO FORCE OF ARMS...
...BUT TREACHERY-- NOW THAT'S SOMETHING ELSE AGAIN.
HOW DO WE GET IN?
SIMPLE. I RING THE DOOR BELL...
...AN' WE WAIT FOR MR. O'DONNELL T' LOWER THE DRAWBRIDGE.
SO, COUSIN, YOU'VE COME AFTER ALL. AND BROUGHT FRIENDS WITH YOU, IT SEEMS.
FIVE FLIES, WINGING THEIR WAYS INTO BLACK TOM'S WEB-- NEVER TO ESCAPE ALIVE.

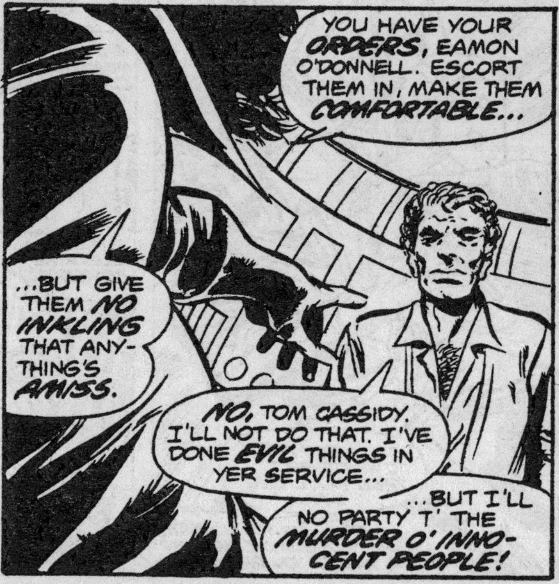
YOU HAVE YOUR ORDERS, EAMON O'DONNELL. ESCORT THEM IN, MAKE THEM COMFORTABLE...
...BUT GIVE THEM NO INKLING THAT ANYTHING'S AMISS.
NO, TOM CASSIDY. I'LL NOT DO THAT. I'VE DONE EVIL THINGS IN YER SERVICE...
...BUT I'LL NO PARTY T' THE MURDER O' INNOCENT PEOPLE!

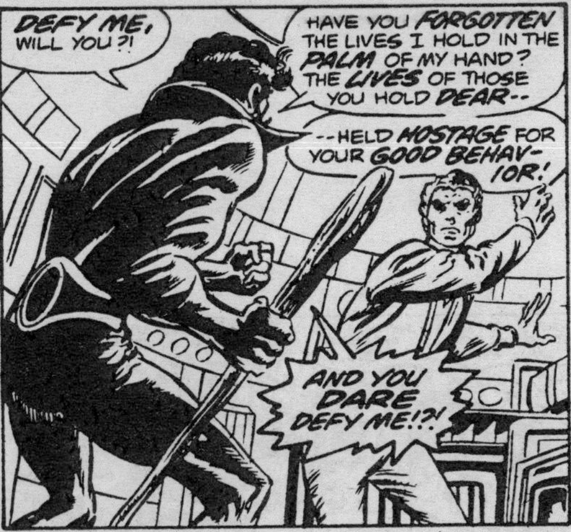
DEFY ME, WILL YOU?!
HAVE YOU FORGOTTEN THE LIVES I HOLD IN THE PALM OF MY HAND? THE LIVES OF THOSE YOU HOLD DEAR--
--HELD HOSTAGE FOR YOUR GOOD BEHAVIOR!
AND YOU DARE DEFY ME!?!

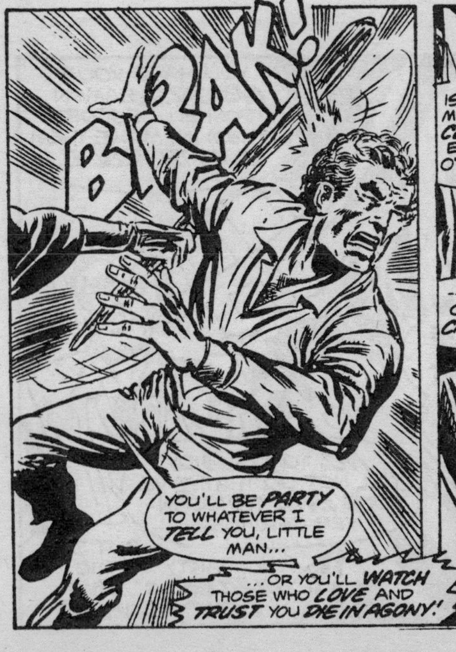
BRAK!
YOU'LL BE PARTY TO WHATEVER I TELL YOU, LITTLE MAN...
...OR YOU'LL WATCH THOSE WHO LOVE AND TRUST YOU DIE IN AGONY!

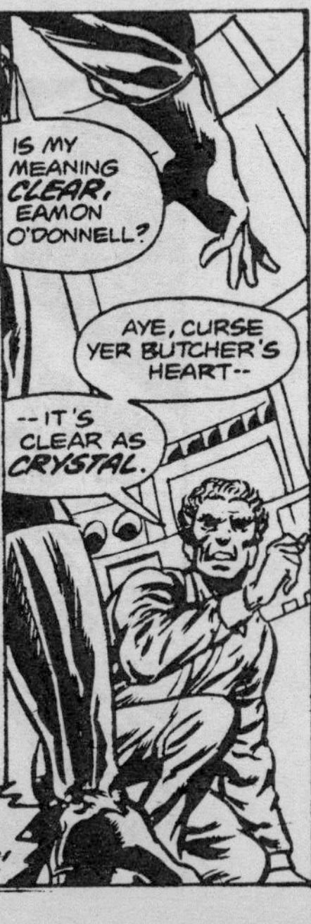
IS MY MEANING CLEAR, EAMON O'DONNELL?
AYE, CURSE YER BUTCHER'S HEART--
--IT'S CLEAR AS CRYSTAL.

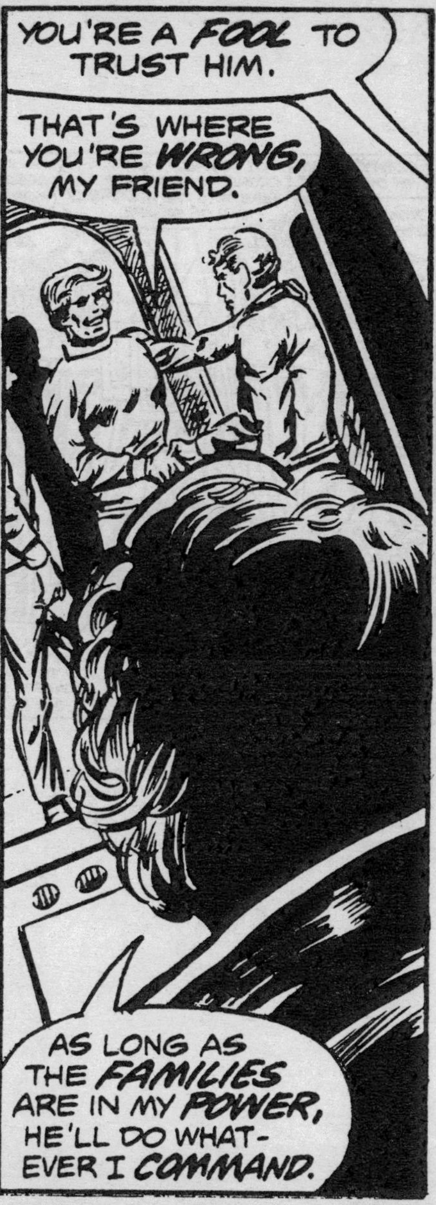
YOU'RE A FOOL TO TRUST HIM.
THAT'S WHERE YOU'RE WRONG, MY FRIEND.
AS LONG AS THE FAMILIES ARE IN MY POWER, HE'LL DO WHAT-EVER I COMMAND.

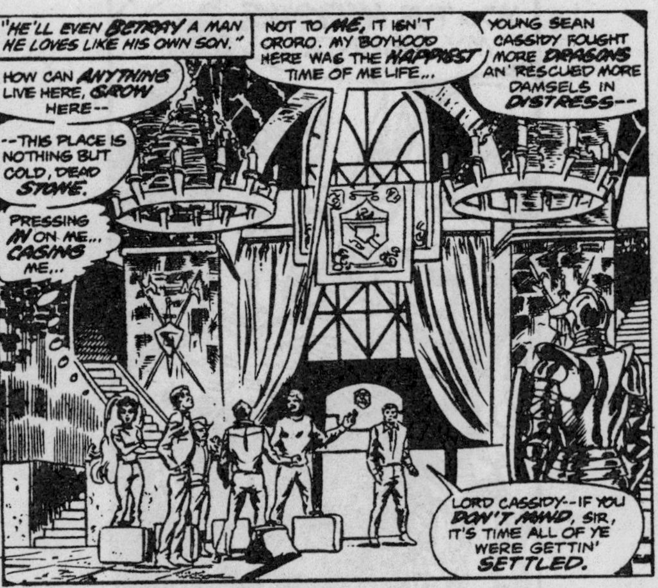
"HE'LL EVEN BETRAY A MAN HE LOVES LIKE HIS OWN SON."
NOT TO ME, IT ISN'T ORORO. MY BOYHOOD HERE WAS THE HAPPIEST TIME OF ME LIFE...
YOUNG SEAN CASSIDY FOUGHT MORE DRAGONS AN' RESCUED MORE DAMSELS IN DISTRESS--
HOW CAN ANYTHING LIVE HERE, GROW HERE--
--THIS PLACE IS NOTHING BUT COLD, DEAD STONE.
PRESSING IN ON ME... CASING ME...
LORD CASSIDY--IF YOU DON'T MIND, SIR, IT'S TIME ALL OF YE WERE GETTIN' SETTLED.

LEAD ON, EAMON.

EAMON O'DONNELL HERE IS THE CASTLE'S *SENESCHAL* -- THE STEWARD O' THE HOUSE. IF YE *NEED* ANYTHING, JUST ASK HIM.

BY THE WAY, OLD FRIEND, *HOW ARE* THE FAMILIES? THE *LITTLE ONES?*

THEY ARE... *WELL,* MILORD.

THIS IS *YER* ROOM, MISS ORORO-- I TRUST IT'S *SATISFACTORY.*

IT SEEMS ALL RIGHT.

VERY WELL. *DINNER* WILL BE SERVED PROMPTLY AT *EIGHT.* THIS WAY, GENTLEMEN.

AH, BANSHEE, YOU'RE SO *HAPPY* TO BE HOME...

...WHILE *I* WILL ONLY BE HAPPY THE DAY I *LEAVE* THIS CASTLE FOREVER.

*JEAN* WOULD SAY CASSIDY KEEP HAS *"BAD VIBES"* FOR ME...

...AND IT *DOES.* BUT I WILL *NOT* BE RULED BY MY *FEARS.* I MUST FORCE MYSELF TO *RELAX...*

AND I KNOW *PRE-CISELY* HOW TO DO IT.

FOR WHEN THE GODDESS OF THE STORM WISHES TO *REFRESH* HERSELF AND *CALM* HER NERVES...

...HOW *BETTER* THAN BY *SUMMONING* HER OWN *SUMMER SHOWER?*

GODS, HOW I *NEEDED* THIS.

IF I *CLOSE* MY EYES, I CAN ALMOST IMAGINE MYSELF BACK IN *KENYA.*

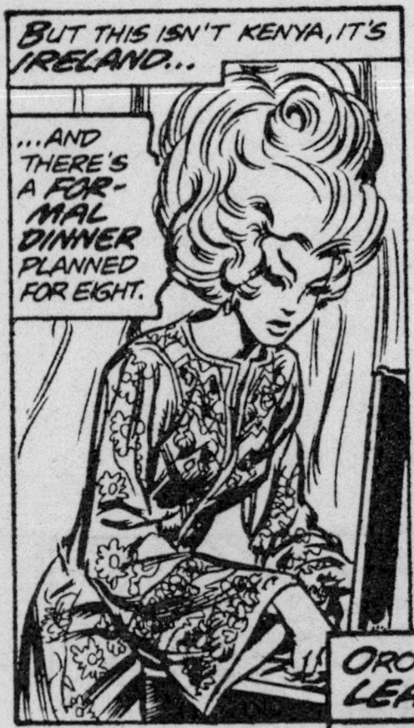
BUT THIS ISN'T KENYA, IT'S IRELAND...
...AND THERE'S A FOR-MAL DINNER PLANNED FOR EIGHT.

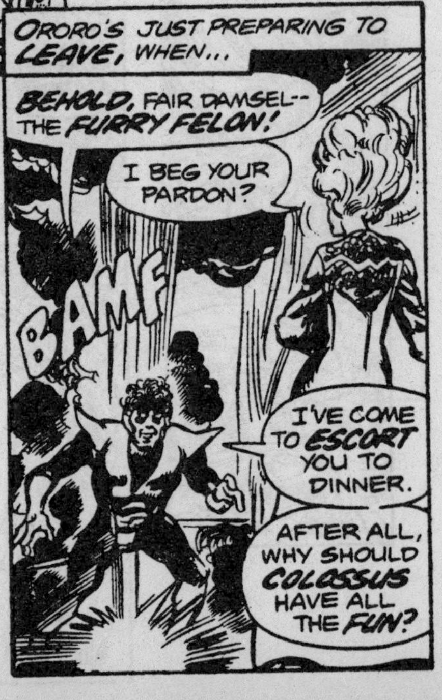
ORORO'S JUST PREPARING TO LEAVE, WHEN...
BEHOLD, FAIR DAMSEL-- THE FURRY FELON!
I BEG YOUR PARDON?
BAMF
I'VE COME TO ESCORT YOU TO DINNER.
AFTER ALL, WHY SHOULD COLOSSUS HAVE ALL THE FUN?

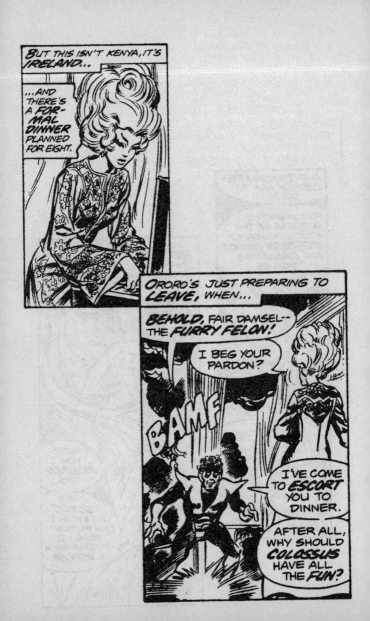

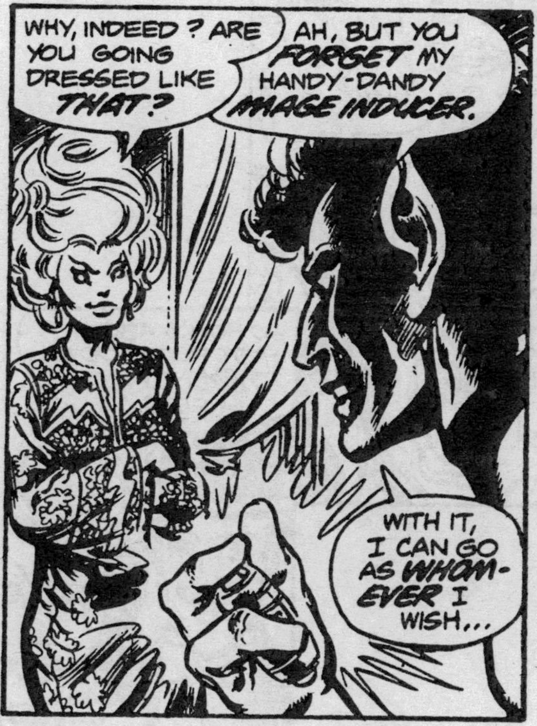
WHY, INDEED? ARE YOU GOING DRESSED LIKE THAT?
AH, BUT YOU FORGET MY HANDY-DANDY IMAGE INDUCER.
WITH IT, I CAN GO AS WHOM-EVER I WISH...

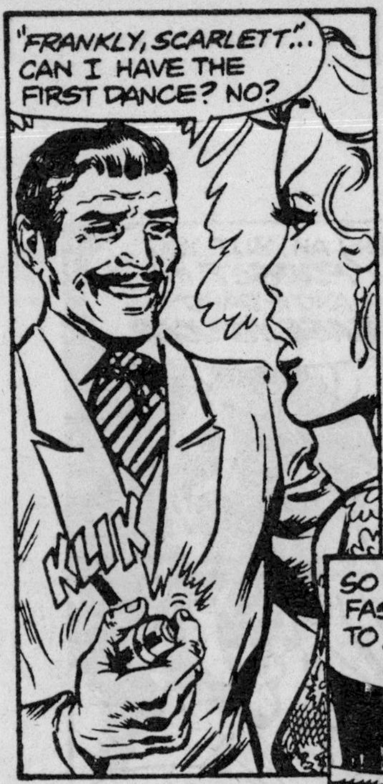
"FRANKLY, SCARLETT"... CAN I HAVE THE FIRST DANCE? NO?
KLIK
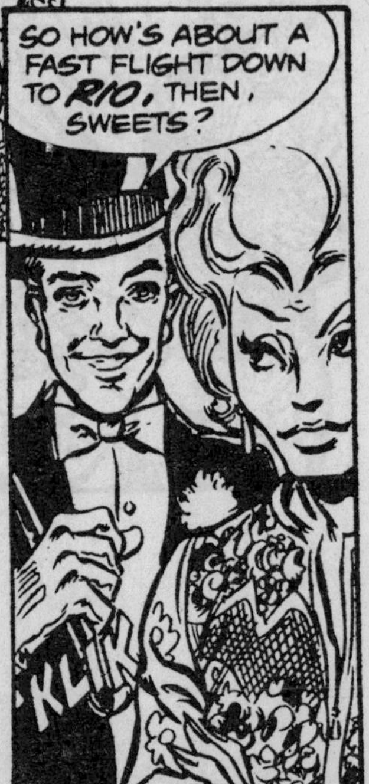
SO HOW'S ABOUT A FAST FLIGHT DOWN TO RIO, THEN, SWEETS?
KLIK

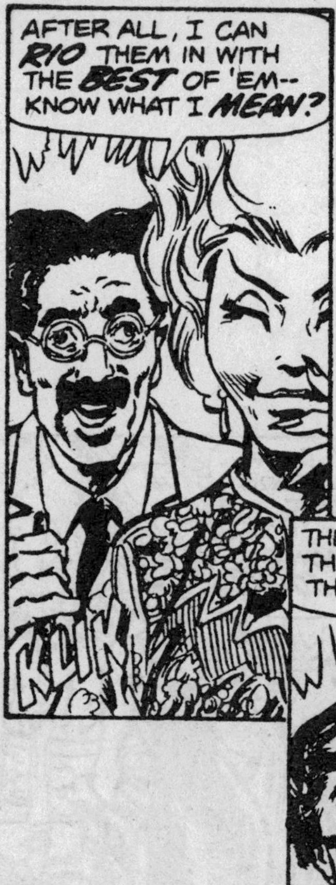
AFTER ALL, I CAN RIO THEM IN WITH THE BEST OF 'EM-- KNOW WHAT I MEAN?
KLIK

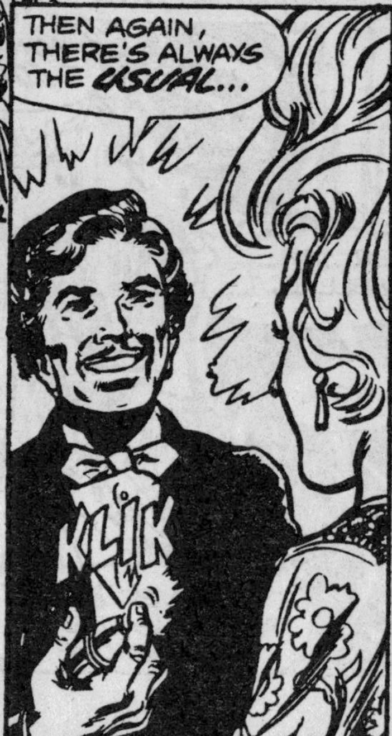
THEN AGAIN, THERE'S ALWAYS THE USUAL...
KLIK

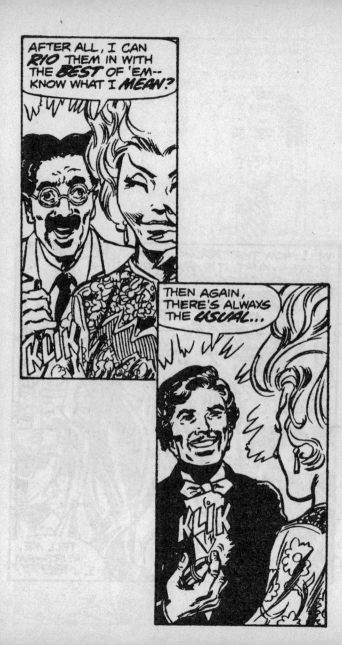

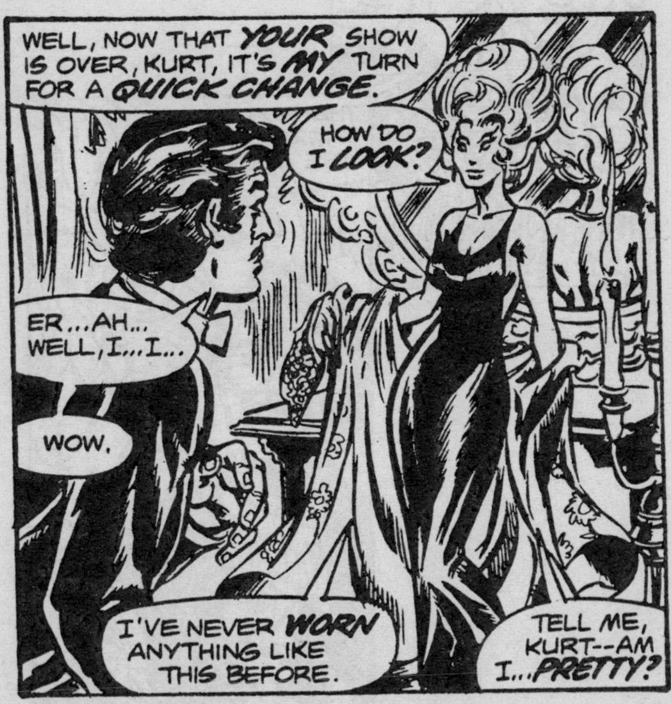
WELL, NOW THAT YOUR SHOW IS OVER, KURT, IT'S MY TURN FOR A QUICK CHANGE.
HOW DO I LOOK?
ER...AH... WELL, I...I...
WOW.
I'VE NEVER WORN ANYTHING LIKE THIS BEFORE.
TELL ME, KURT--AM I...PRETTY?

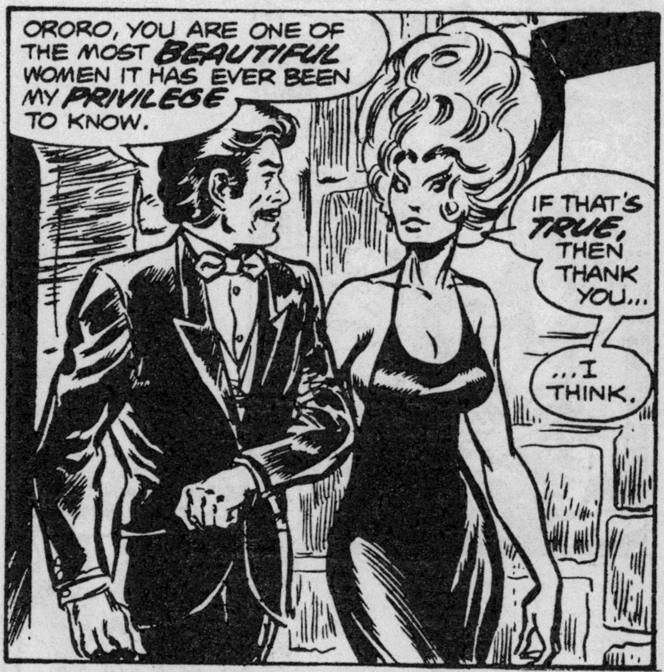
ORORO, YOU ARE ONE OF THE MOST BEAUTIFUL WOMEN IT HAS EVER BEEN MY PRIVILEGE TO KNOW.
IF THAT'S TRUE, THEN THANK YOU...
...I THINK.

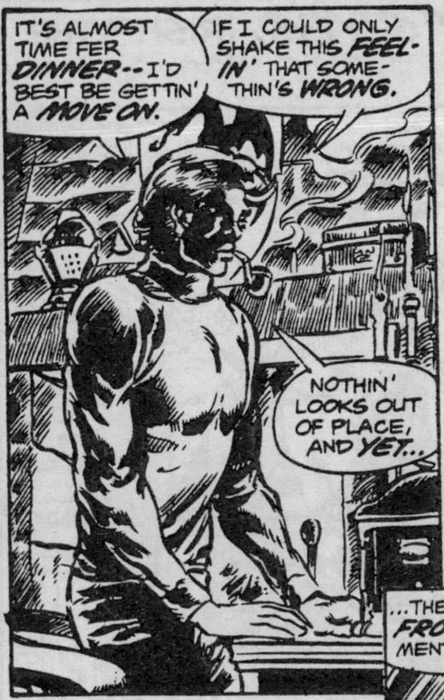
IT'S ALMOST TIME FER DINNER--I'D BEST BE GETTIN' A MOVE ON.
IF I COULD ONLY SHAKE THIS FEEL-IN' THAT SOME-THIN'S WRONG.
NOTHIN' LOOKS OUT OF PLACE, AND YET...

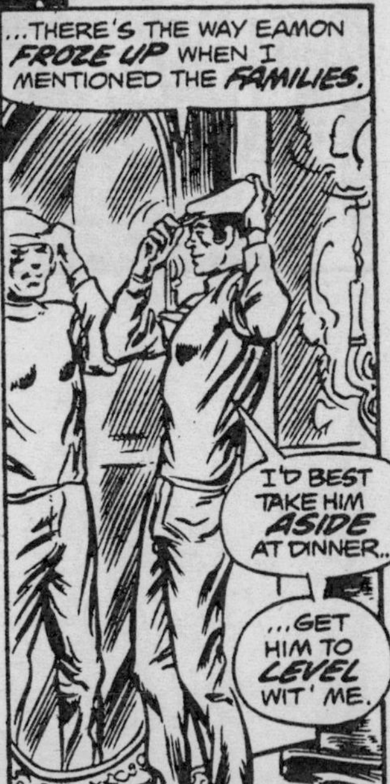
...THERE'S THE WAY EAMON FROZE UP WHEN I MENTIONED THE FAMILIES.
I'D BEST TAKE HIM ASIDE AT DINNER...
...GET HIM TO LEVEL WIT' ME.

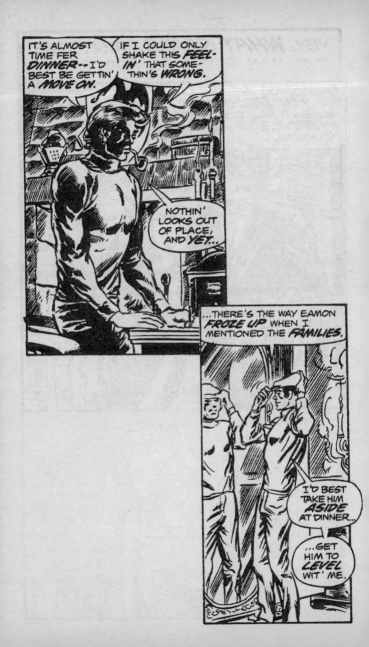

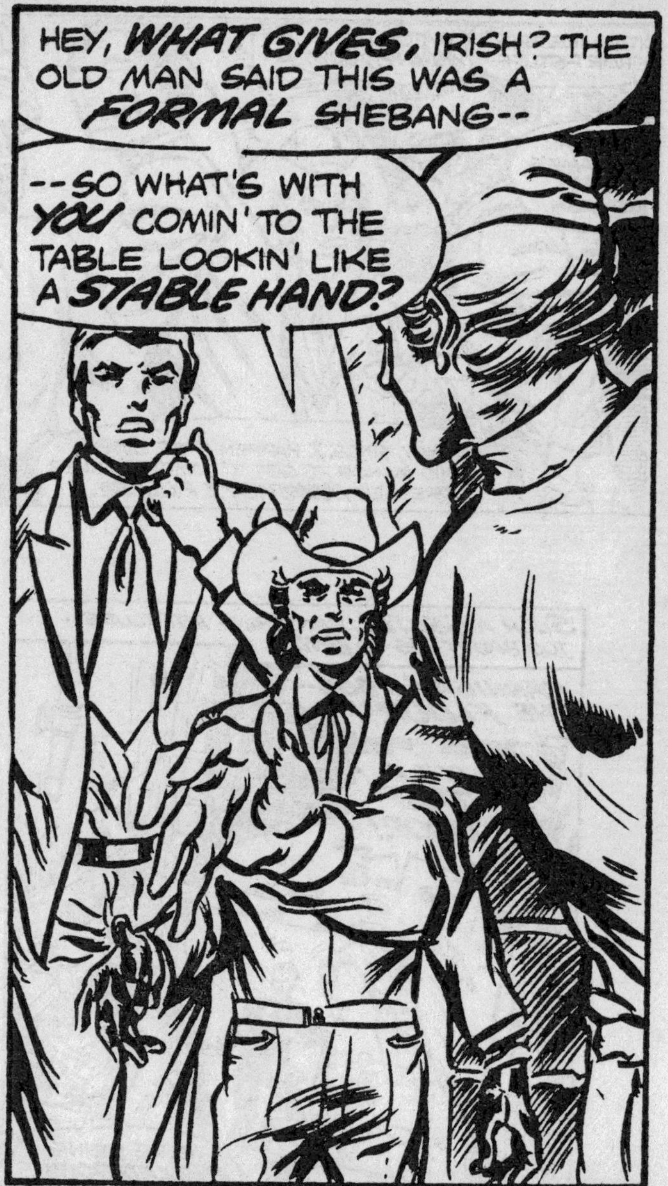
HEY, WHAT GIVES, IRISH? THE OLD MAN SAID THIS WAS A FORMAL SHEBANG--
--SO WHAT'S WITH YOU COMIN' TO THE TABLE LOOKIN' LIKE A STABLE HAND?

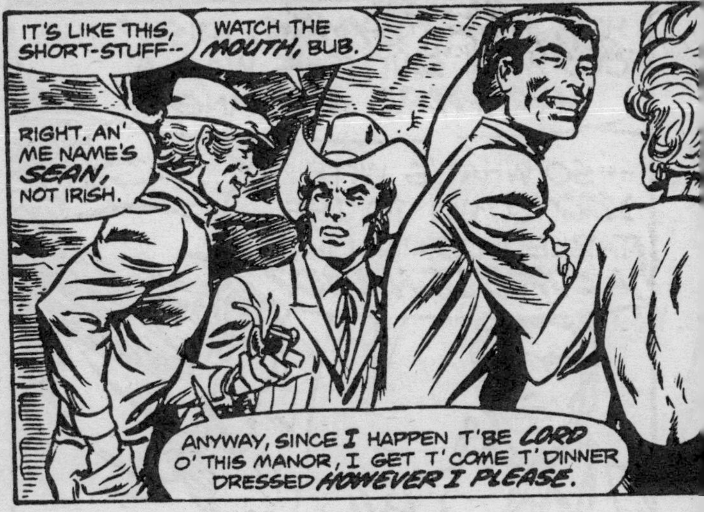
IT'S LIKE THIS, SHORT-STUFF--
WATCH THE MOUTH, BUB.
RIGHT. AN' ME NAME'S SEAN, NOT IRISH.
ANYWAY, SINCE I HAPPEN T'BE LORD O' THIS MANOR, I GET T'COME T'DINNER DRESSED HOWEVER I PLEASE.

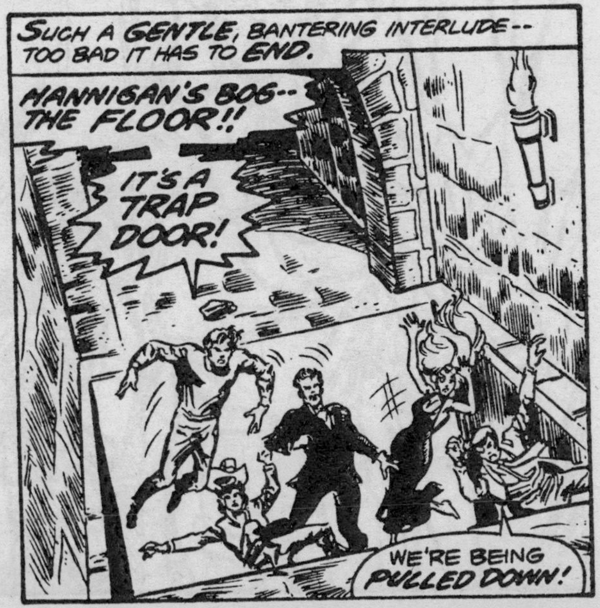
SUCH A GENTLE, BANTERING INTERLUDE-- TOO BAD IT HAS TO END.
MANNIGAN'S BOG-- THE FLOOR!!
IT'S A TRAP DOOR!
WE'RE BEING PULLED DOWN!

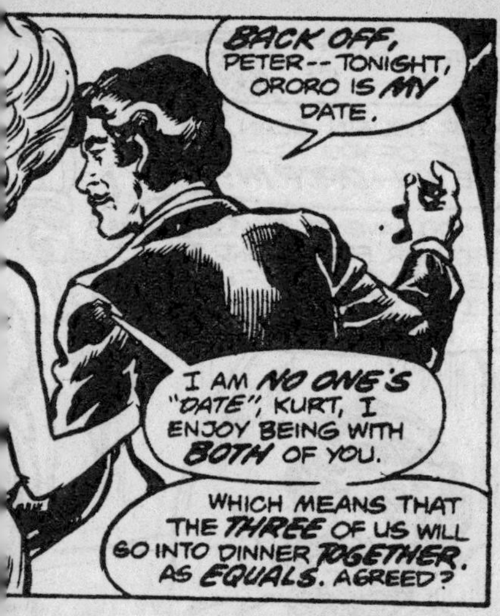
BACK OFF, PETER--TONIGHT, ORORO IS MY DATE.
I AM NO ONE'S "DATE", KURT, I ENJOY BEING WITH BOTH OF YOU.
WHICH MEANS THAT THE THREE OF US WILL GO INTO DINNER TOGETHER. AS EQUALS. AGREED?

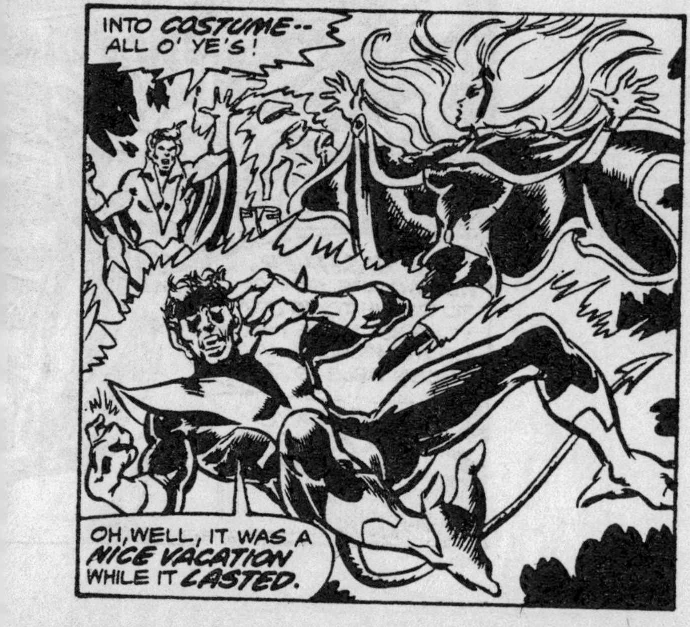
INTO COSTUME-- ALL O' YE'S!
OH, WELL, IT WAS A NICE VACATION WHILE IT LASTED.

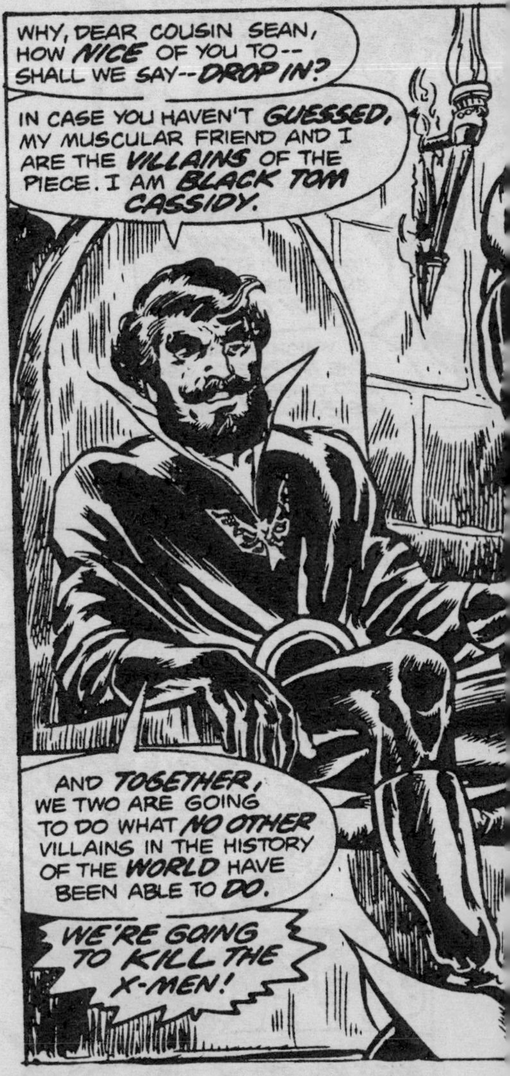
WHY, DEAR COUSIN SEAN, HOW NICE OF YOU TO-- SHALL WE SAY--DROP IN?
IN CASE YOU HAVEN'T GUESSED, MY MUSCULAR FRIEND AND I ARE THE VILLAINS OF THE PIECE. I AM BLACK TOM CASSIDY.
AND TOGETHER, WE TWO ARE GOING TO DO WHAT NO OTHER VILLAINS IN THE HISTORY OF THE WORLD HAVE BEEN ABLE TO DO.
WE'RE GOING TO KILL THE X-MEN!

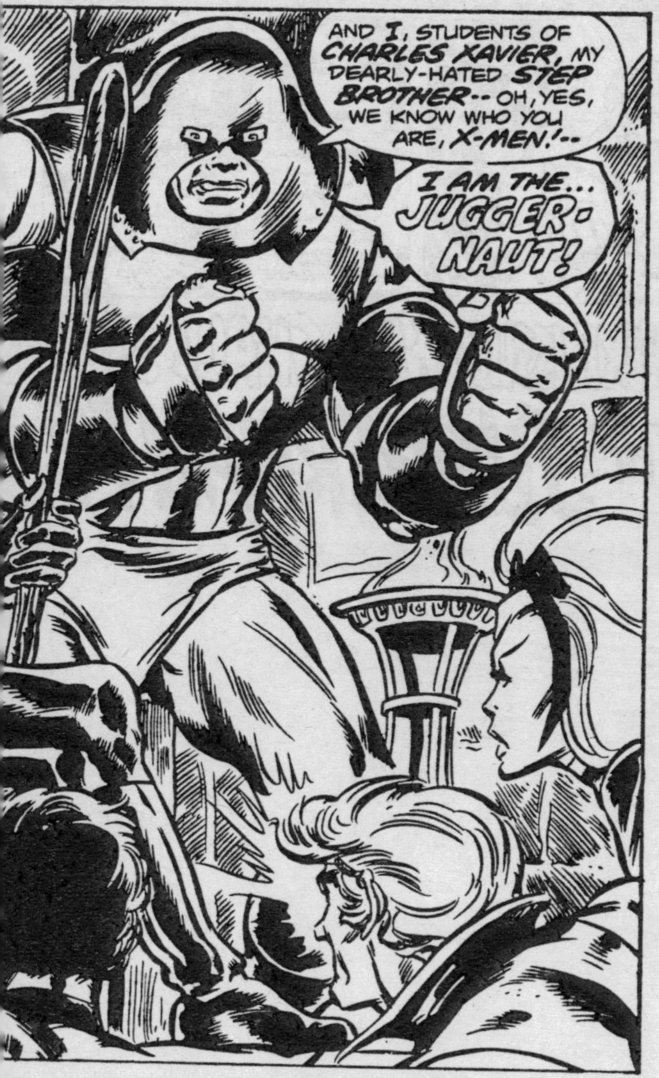
AND I, STUDENTS OF CHARLES XAVIER, MY DEARLY-HATED STEP BROTHER-- OH, YES, WE KNOW WHO YOU ARE, X-MEN!--
I AM THE... JUGGER-NAUT!

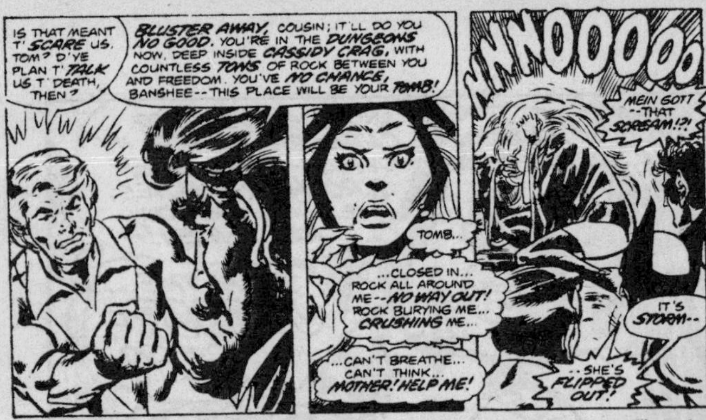
IS THAT MEANT T' SCARE US, TOM? D'YE PLAN T' TALK US T' DEATH, THEN?
BLUSTER AWAY, COUSIN; IT'LL DO YOU NO GOOD. YOU'RE IN THE DUNGEONS NOW, DEEP INSIDE CASSIDY CRAG, WITH COUNTLESS TONS OF ROCK BETWEEN YOU AND FREEDOM. YOU'VE NO CHANCE, BANSHEE--THIS PLACE WILL BE YOUR TOMB!
TOMB...
...CLOSED IN... ROCK ALL AROUND ME--NO WAY OUT! ROCK BURYING ME... CRUSHING ME...
...CAN'T BREATHE... CAN'T THINK... MOTHER! HELP ME!
NNNOOOOOo
MEIN GOTT --THAT SCREAM!?!
IT'S STORM--
--SHE'S FLIPPED OUT!

# NEXT ISSUE: WHO SHALL STOP THE JUGGERNAUT?

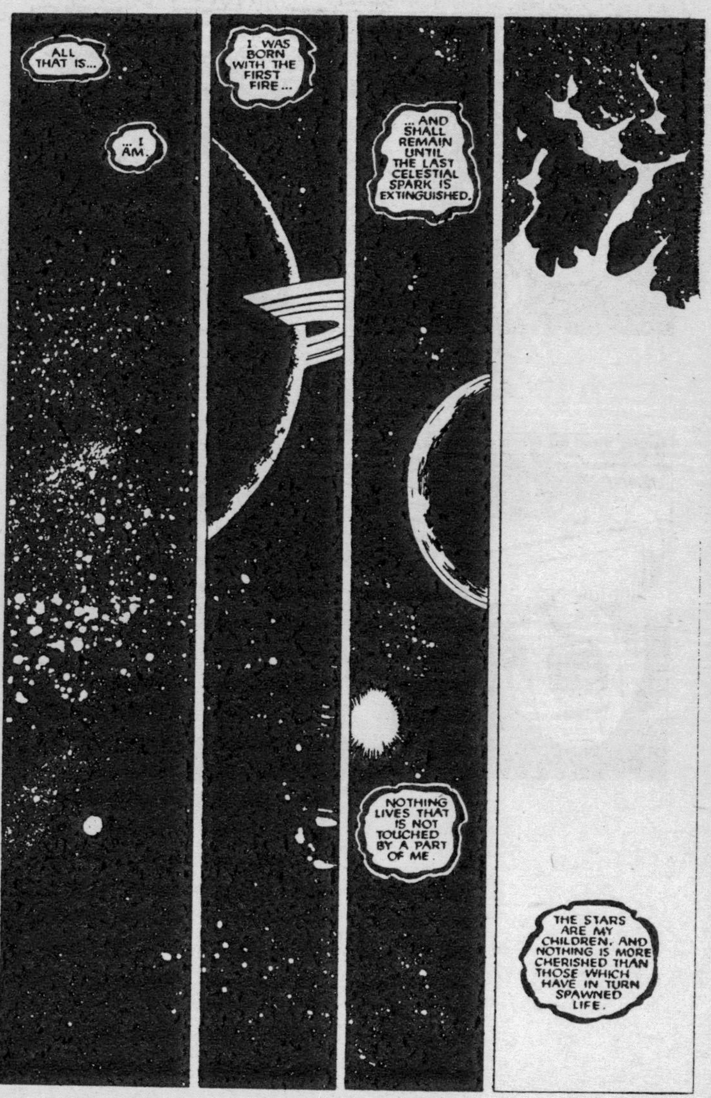
ALL THAT IS...
... I AM.
I WAS BORN WITH THE FIRST FIRE...
... AND SHALL REMAIN UNTIL THE LAST CELESTIAL SPARK IS EXTINGUISHED.
NOTHING LIVES THAT IS NOT TOUCHED BY A PART OF ME.
THE STARS ARE MY CHILDREN, AND NOTHING IS MORE CHERISHED THAN THOSE WHICH HAVE IN TURN SPAWNED LIFE.

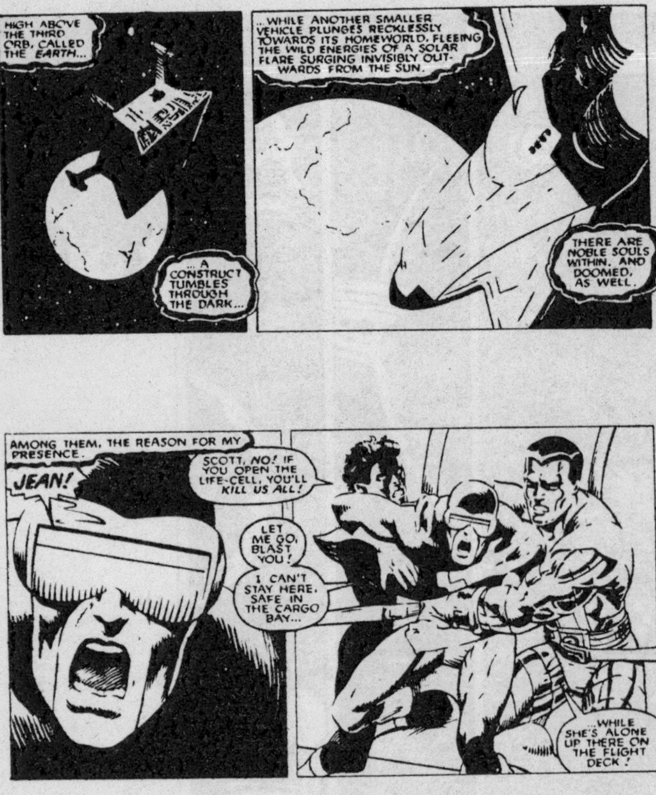
HIGH ABOVE THE THIRD ORB, CALLED THE EARTH...
...A CONSTRUCT TUMBLES THROUGH THE DARK...
...WHILE ANOTHER SMALLER VEHICLE PLUNGES RECKLESSLY TOWARDS ITS HOMEWORLD, FLEEING THE WILD ENERGIES OF A SOLAR FLARE SURGING INVISIBLY OUT-WARDS FROM THE SUN.
THERE ARE NOBLE SOULS WITHIN. AND DOOMED, AS WELL.
AMONG THEM, THE REASON FOR MY PRESENCE.
JEAN!
SCOTT, NO! IF YOU OPEN THE LIFE-CELL, YOU'LL KILL US ALL!
LET ME GO, BLAST YOU!
I CAN'T STAY HERE, SAFE IN THE CARGO BAY...
...WHILE SHE'S ALONE UP THERE ON THE FLIGHT DECK!

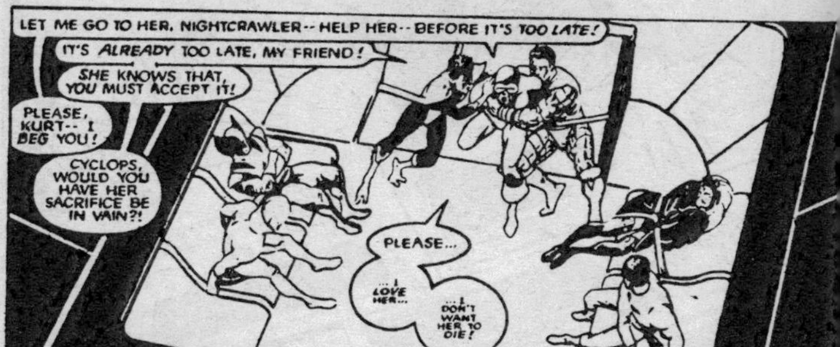
LET ME GO TO HER, NIGHTCRAWLER-- HELP HER-- BEFORE IT'S TOO LATE!
IT'S ALREADY TOO LATE, MY FRIEND!
SHE KNOWS THAT, YOU MUST ACCEPT IT!
PLEASE, KURT-- I BEG YOU!
CYCLOPS, WOULD YOU HAVE HER SACRIFICE BE IN VAIN?!
PLEASE...
...I LOVE HER...
...I DON'T WANT HER TO DIE!

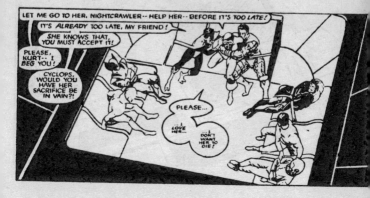

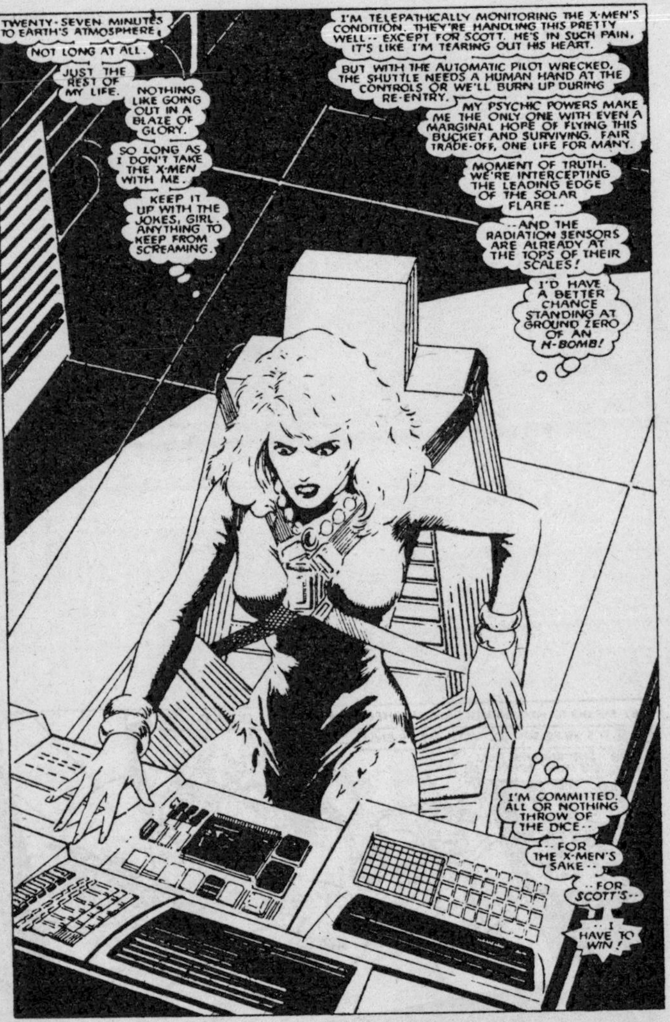
TWENTY-SEVEN MINUTES TO EARTH'S ATMOSPHERE.
NOT LONG AT ALL.
JUST THE REST OF MY LIFE.
NOTHING LIKE GOING OUT IN A BLAZE OF GLORY.
SO LONG AS I DON'T TAKE THE X-MEN WITH ME.
KEEP IT UP WITH THE JOKES, GIRL. ANYTHING TO KEEP FROM SCREAMING.
I'M TELEPATHICALLY MONITORING THE X-MEN'S CONDITION. THEY'RE HANDLING THIS PRETTY WELL -- EXCEPT FOR SCOTT. HE'S IN SUCH PAIN, IT'S LIKE I'M TEARING OUT HIS HEART.
BUT WITH THE AUTOMATIC PILOT WRECKED, THE SHUTTLE NEEDS A HUMAN HAND AT THE CONTROLS OR WE'LL BURN UP DURING RE-ENTRY.
MY PSYCHIC POWERS MAKE ME THE ONLY ONE WITH EVEN A MARGINAL HOPE OF FLYING THIS BUCKET AND SURVIVING. FAIR TRADE-OFF, ONE LIFE FOR MANY.
MOMENT OF TRUTH. WE'RE INTERCEPTING THE LEADING EDGE OF THE SOLAR FLARE --
-- AND THE RADIATION SENSORS ARE ALREADY AT THE TOPS OF THEIR SCALES!
I'D HAVE A BETTER CHANCE STANDING AT GROUND ZERO OF AN H-BOMB!
I'M COMMITTED. ALL OR NOTHING THROW OF THE DICE --
-- FOR THE X-MEN'S SAKE --
-- FOR SCOTT'S --
-- I HAVE TO WIN!

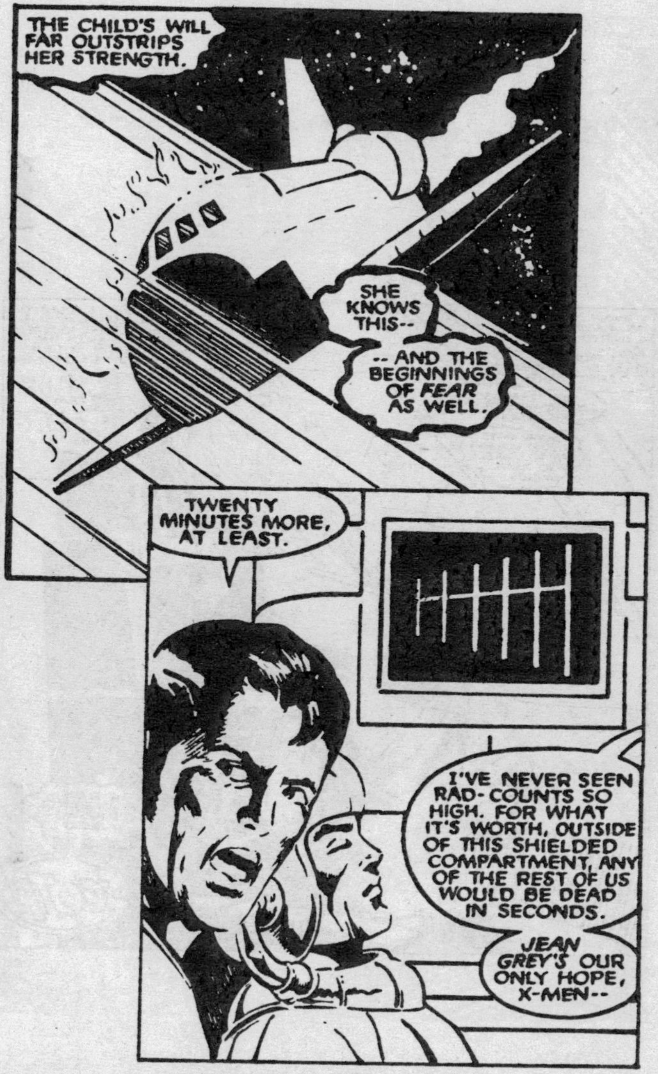
THE CHILD'S WILL FAR OUTSTRIPS HER STRENGTH.
SHE KNOWS THIS--
-- AND THE BEGINNINGS OF *FEAR* AS WELL.
TWENTY MINUTES MORE, AT LEAST.
I'VE NEVER SEEN RAD-COUNTS SO HIGH. FOR WHAT IT'S WORTH, OUTSIDE OF THIS SHIELDED COMPARTMENT, ANY OF THE REST OF US WOULD BE DEAD IN SECONDS.
*JEAN GREY'S* OUR ONLY HOPE, X-MEN--

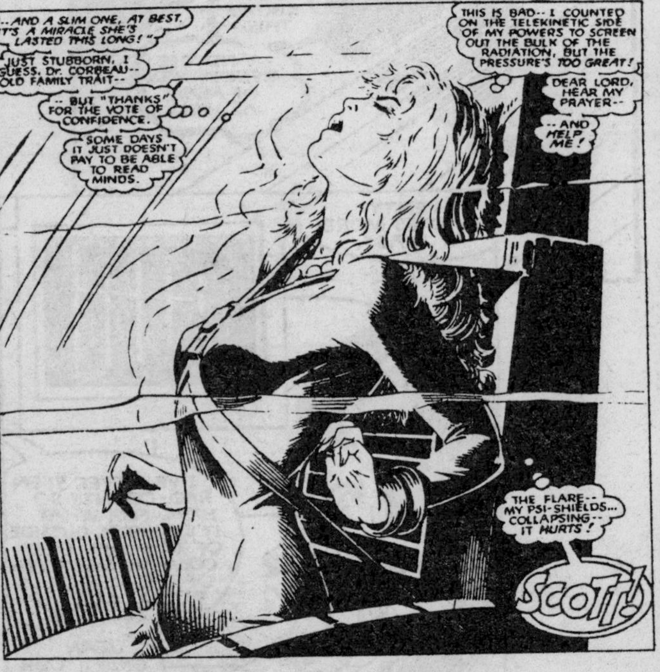
"..AND A SLIM ONE, AT BEST. IT'S A MIRACLE SHE'S LASTED THIS LONG!"
JUST STUBBORN, I GUESS, Dr. CORBEAU-- OLD FAMILY TRAIT--
-- BUT "THANKS" FOR THE VOTE OF CONFIDENCE.
SOME DAYS IT JUST DOESN'T PAY TO BE ABLE TO READ MINDS.
THIS IS BAD-- I COUNTED ON THE TELEKINETIC SIDE OF MY POWERS TO SCREEN OUT THE BULK OF THE RADIATION, BUT THE PRESSURE'S TOO GREAT!
DEAR LORD, HEAR MY PRAYER--
-- AND HELP ME!
THE FLARE-- MY PSI-SHIELDS... COLLAPSING-- IT HURTS!
SCOTT!

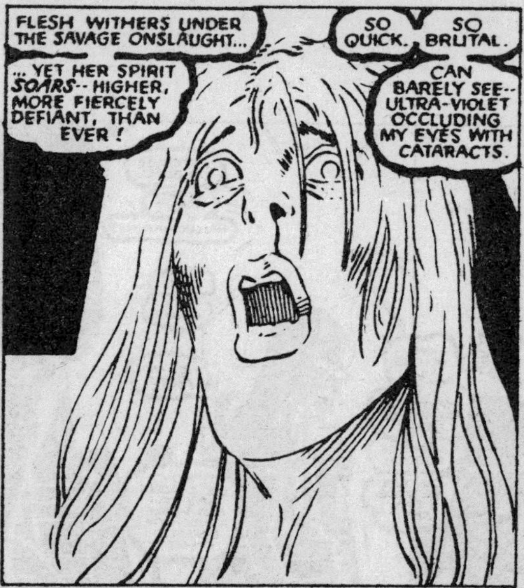
FLESH WITHERS UNDER THE SAVAGE ONSLAUGHT...
... YET HER SPIRIT SOARS-- HIGHER, MORE FIERCELY DEFIANT, THAN EVER!
SO QUICK.
SO BRUTAL.
CAN BARELY SEE-- ULTRA-VIOLET OCCLUDING MY EYES WITH CATARACTS.

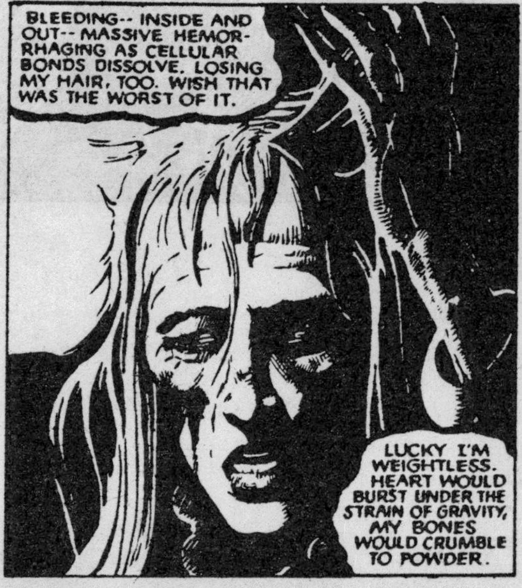
BLEEDING-- INSIDE AND OUT-- MASSIVE HEMORRHAGING AS CELLULAR BONDS DISSOLVE. LOSING MY HAIR, TOO. WISH THAT WAS THE WORST OF IT.
LUCKY I'M WEIGHTLESS. HEART WOULD BURST UNDER THE STRAIN OF GRAVITY, MY BONES WOULD CRUMBLE TO POWDER.

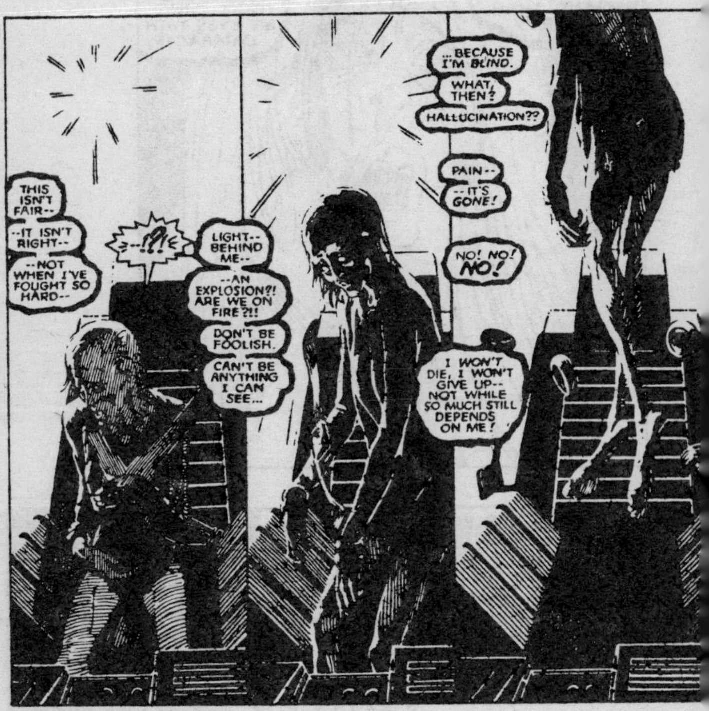
THIS ISN'T FAIR--
--IT ISN'T RIGHT--
--NOT WHEN I'VE FOUGHT SO HARD--
--!?!--
LIGHT-- BEHIND ME--
--AN EXPLOSION?! ARE WE ON FIRE?!!
DON'T BE FOOLISH.
CAN'T BE ANYTHING I CAN SEE...
...BECAUSE I'M BLIND.
WHAT, THEN?
HALLUCINATION??
PAIN--
--IT'S GONE!
NO! NO! NO!
I WON'T DIE, I WON'T GIVE UP-- NOT WHILE SO MUCH STILL DEPENDS ON ME!

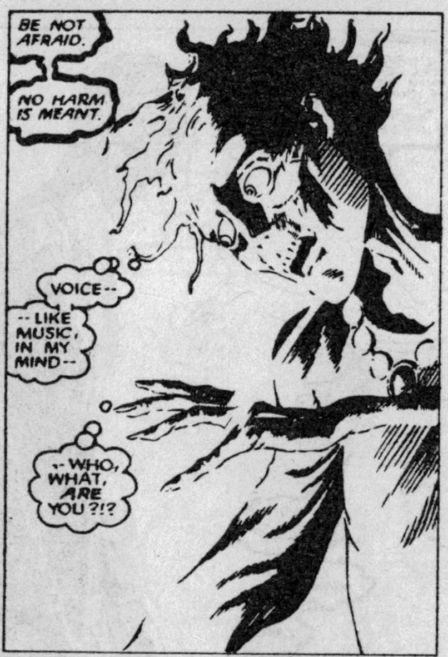
BE NOT AFRAID.
NO HARM IS MEANT.
VOICE--
--LIKE MUSIC, IN MY MIND--
--WHO, WHAT, ARE YOU?!?

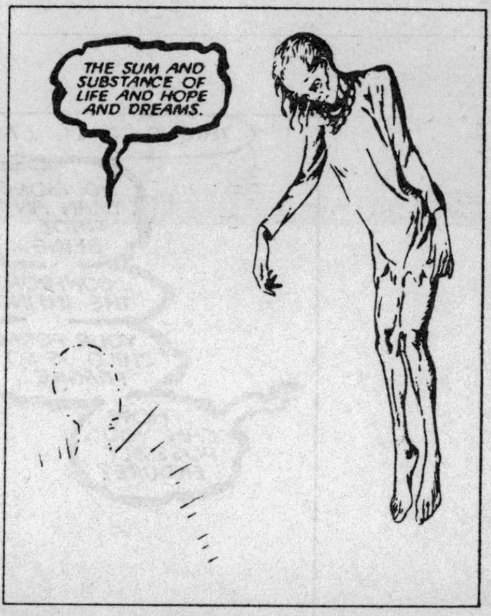
THE SUM AND SUBSTANCE OF LIFE AND HOPE AND DREAMS.

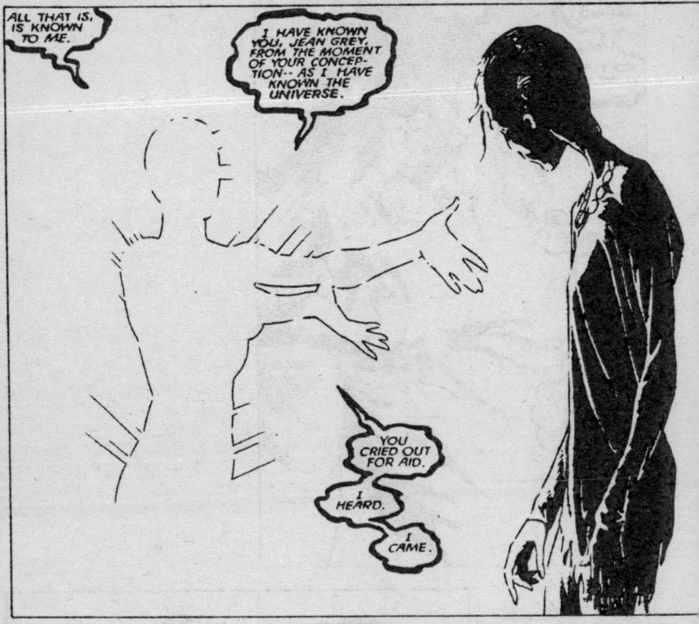
ALL THAT IS, IS KNOWN TO ME.
I HAVE KNOWN YOU, JEAN GREY, FROM THE MOMENT OF YOUR CONCEPTION-- AS I HAVE KNOWN THE UNIVERSE.
YOU CRIED OUT FOR AID.
I HEARD.
I CAME.

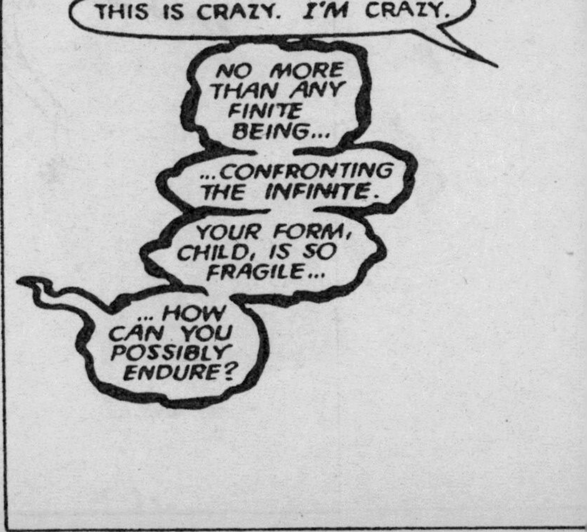
THIS IS CRAZY. I'M CRAZY.
NO MORE THAN ANY FINITE BEING...
...CONFRONTING THE INFINITE.
YOUR FORM, CHILD, IS SO FRAGILE...
...HOW CAN YOU POSSIBLY ENDURE?

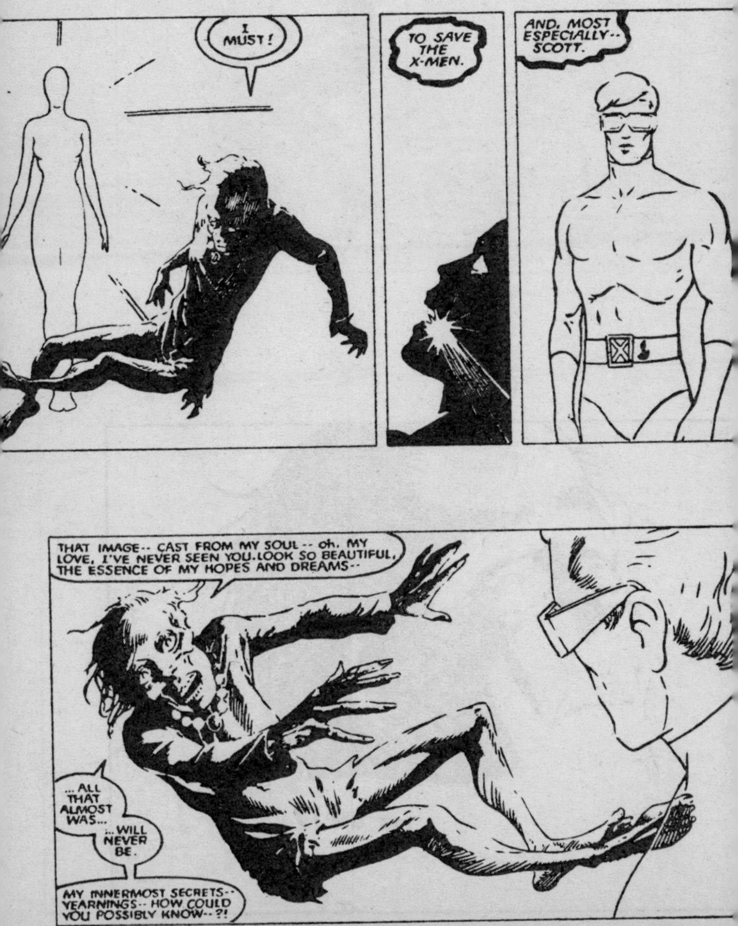
I MUST!
TO SAVE THE X-MEN.
AND, MOST ESPECIALLY-- SCOTT.
THAT IMAGE-- CAST FROM MY SOUL-- oh, MY LOVE, I'VE NEVER SEEN YOU LOOK SO BEAUTIFUL, THE ESSENCE OF MY HOPES AND DREAMS--
...ALL THAT ALMOST WAS... ...WILL NEVER BE.
MY INNERMOST SECRETS-- YEARNINGS-- HOW COULD YOU POSSIBLY KNOW--?!

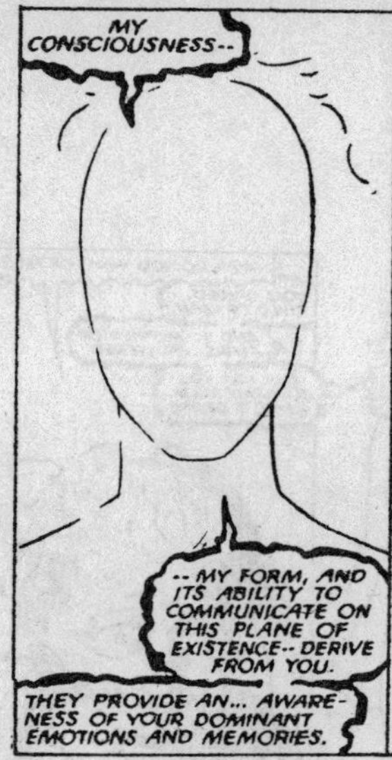
MY CONSCIOUSNESS--
-- MY FORM, AND ITS ABILITY TO COMMUNICATE ON THIS PLANE OF EXISTENCE-- DERIVE FROM YOU.
THEY PROVIDE AN... AWARENESS OF YOUR DOMINANT EMOTIONS AND MEMORIES.

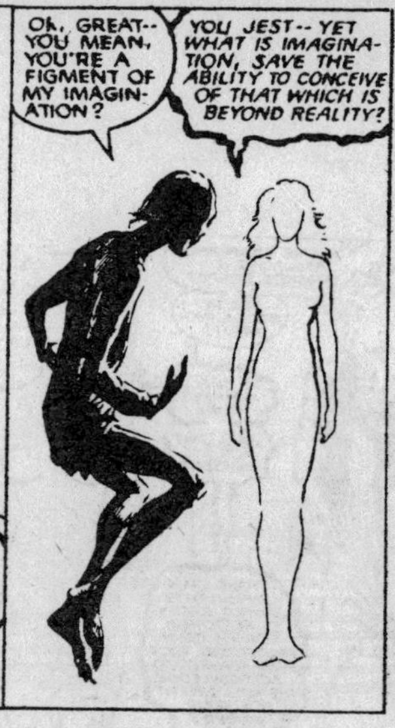
OH, GREAT-- YOU MEAN, YOU'RE A FIGMENT OF MY IMAGINATION?
YOU JEST -- YET WHAT IS IMAGINATION, SAVE THE ABILITY TO CONCEIVE OF THAT WHICH IS BEYOND REALITY?

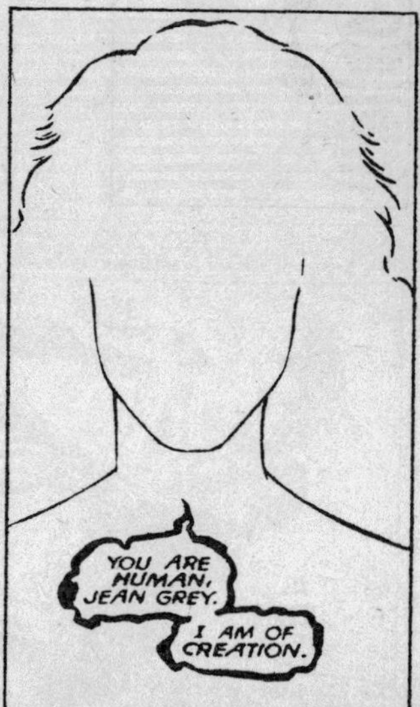
YOU ARE HUMAN, JEAN GREY.
I AM OF CREATION.

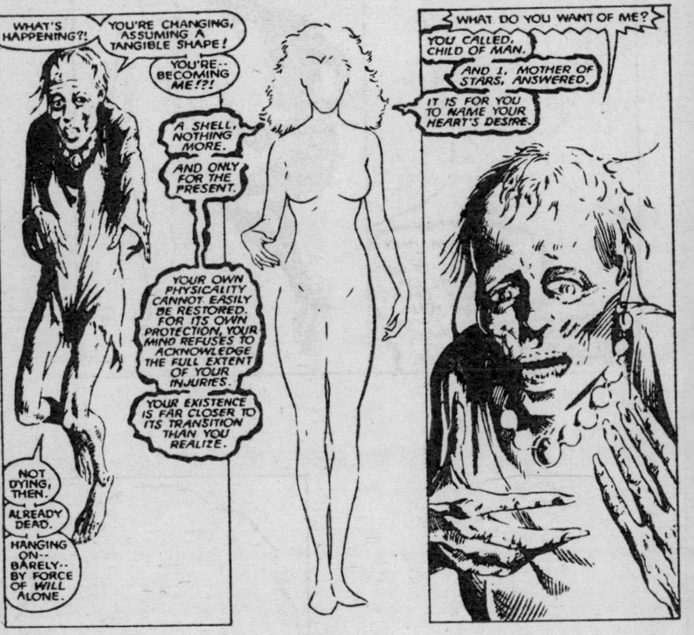
WHAT'S HAPPENING?!
YOU'RE CHANGING, ASSUMING A TANGIBLE SHAPE!
YOU'RE-- BECOMING ME!?!
A SHELL, NOTHING MORE.
AND ONLY FOR THE PRESENT.
YOUR OWN PHYSICALITY CANNOT EASILY BE RESTORED. FOR ITS OWN PROTECTION, YOUR MIND REFUSES TO ACKNOWLEDGE THE FULL EXTENT OF YOUR INJURIES.
YOUR EXISTENCE IS FAR CLOSER TO ITS TRANSITION THAN YOU REALIZE.
NOT DYING, THEN.
ALREADY DEAD.
HANGING ON-- BARELY-- BY FORCE OF WILL ALONE.
WHAT DO YOU WANT OF ME?
YOU CALLED, CHILD OF MAN.
AND I, MOTHER OF STARS, ANSWERED.
IT IS FOR YOU TO NAME YOUR HEART'S DESIRE.

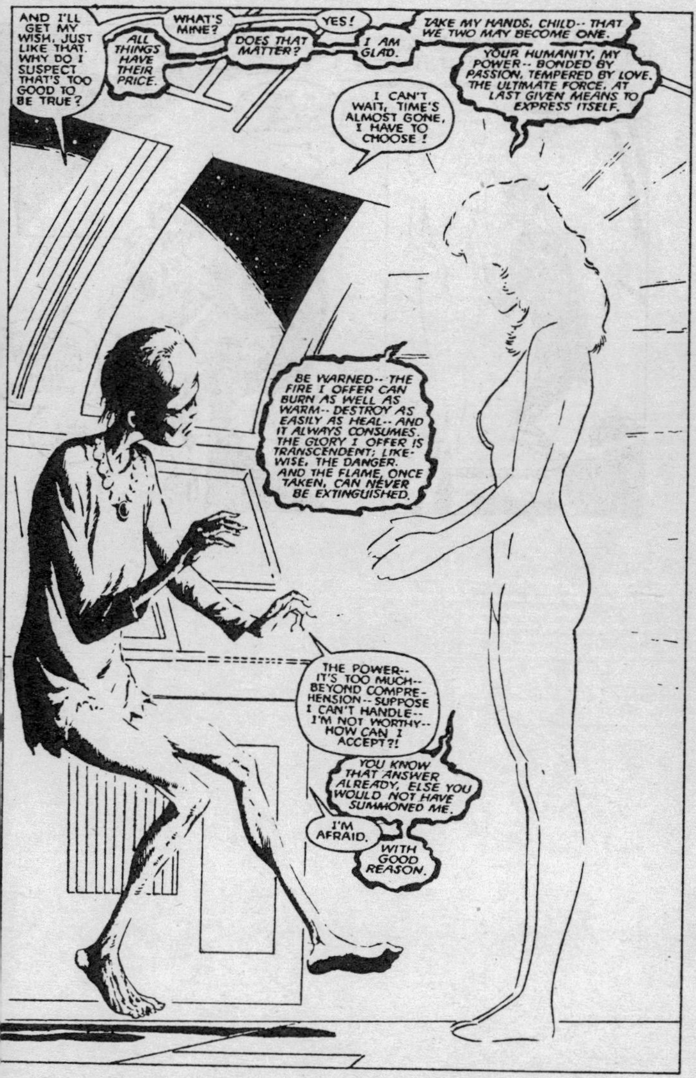
AND I'LL GET MY WISH, JUST LIKE THAT. WHY DO I SUSPECT THAT'S TOO GOOD TO BE TRUE?
ALL THINGS HAVE THEIR PRICE.
WHAT'S MINE?
DOES THAT MATTER?
YES!
I AM GLAD.
TAKE MY HANDS, CHILD-- THAT WE TWO MAY BECOME ONE.
YOUR HUMANITY, MY POWER-- BONDED BY PASSION, TEMPERED BY LOVE. THE ULTIMATE FORCE, AT LAST GIVEN MEANS TO EXPRESS ITSELF.
I CAN'T WAIT, TIME'S ALMOST GONE, I HAVE TO CHOOSE!
BE WARNED-- THE FIRE I OFFER CAN BURN AS WELL AS WARM-- DESTROY AS EASILY AS HEAL-- AND IT ALWAYS CONSUMES. THE GLORY I OFFER IS TRANSCENDENT; LIKEWISE, THE DANGER. AND THE FLAME, ONCE TAKEN, CAN NEVER BE EXTINGUISHED.
THE POWER-- IT'S TOO MUCH-- BEYOND COMPREHENSION-- SUPPOSE I CAN'T HANDLE-- I'M NOT WORTHY-- HOW CAN I ACCEPT?!
YOU KNOW THAT ANSWER ALREADY, ELSE YOU WOULD NOT HAVE SUMMONED ME.
I'M AFRAID.
WITH GOOD REASON.

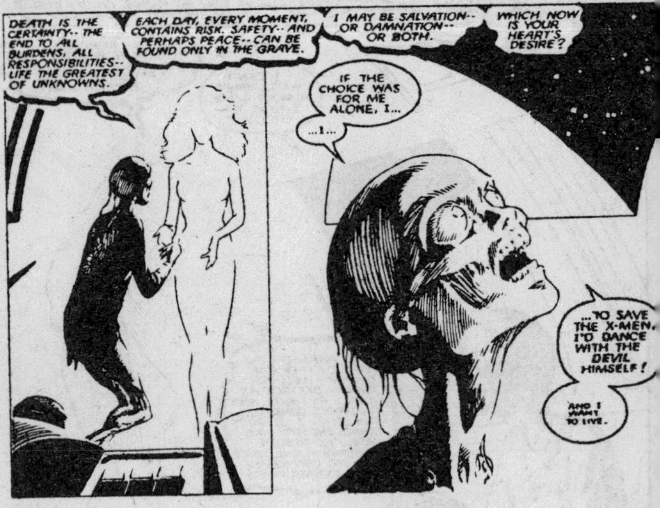
DEATH IS THE CERTAINTY-- THE END TO ALL BURDENS, ALL RESPONSIBILITIES-- LIFE THE GREATEST OF UNKNOWNS.
EACH DAY, EVERY MOMENT, CONTAINS RISK. SAFETY-- AND PERHAPS PEACE-- CAN BE FOUND ONLY IN THE GRAVE.
I MAY BE SALVATION-- OR DAMNATION-- OR BOTH.
WHICH NOW IS YOUR HEART'S DESIRE?
IF THE CHOICE WAS FOR ME ALONE, I...
...I...
...TO SAVE THE X-MEN, I'D DANCE WITH THE DEVIL HIMSELF!
AND I WANT TO LIVE.

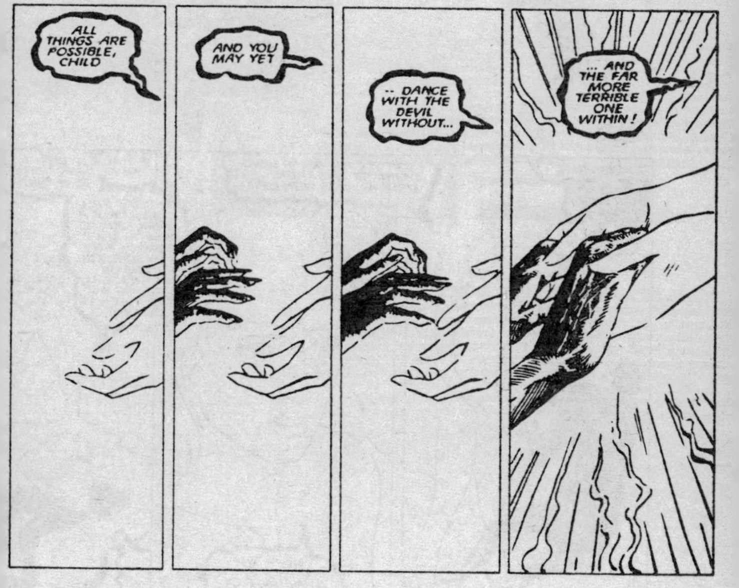
ALL THINGS ARE POSSIBLE, CHILD
AND YOU MAY YET
-- DANCE WITH THE DEVIL WITHOUT...
... AND THE FAR MORE TERRIBLE ONE WITHIN!

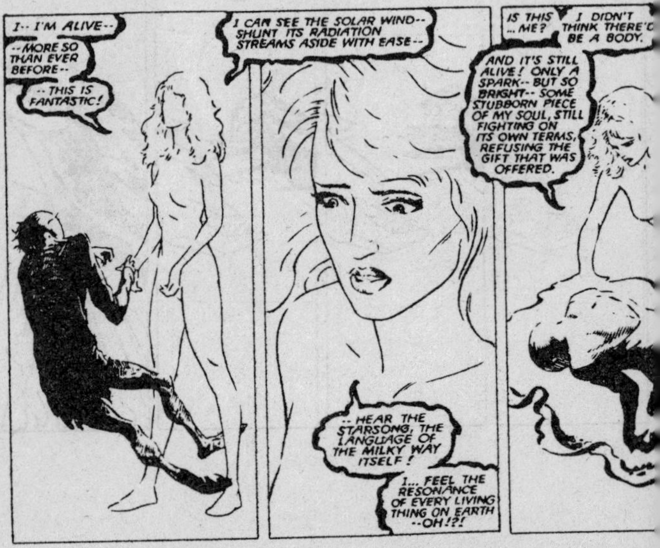

I-- I'M ALIVE--
--MORE SO THAN EVER BEFORE--
--THIS IS FANTASTIC!
I CAN SEE THE SOLAR WIND-- SHUNT ITS RADIATION STREAMS ASIDE WITH EASE--
--HEAR THE STARSONG, THE LANGUAGE OF THE MILKY WAY ITSELF!
I... FEEL THE RESONANCE OF EVERY LIVING THING ON EARTH --OH!?!
IS THIS ...ME?
I DIDN'T THINK THERE'D BE A BODY.
AND IT'S STILL ALIVE! ONLY A SPARK-- BUT SO BRIGHT-- SOME STUBBORN PIECE OF MY SOUL, STILL FIGHTING ON ITS OWN TERMS, REFUSING THE GIFT THAT WAS OFFERED.

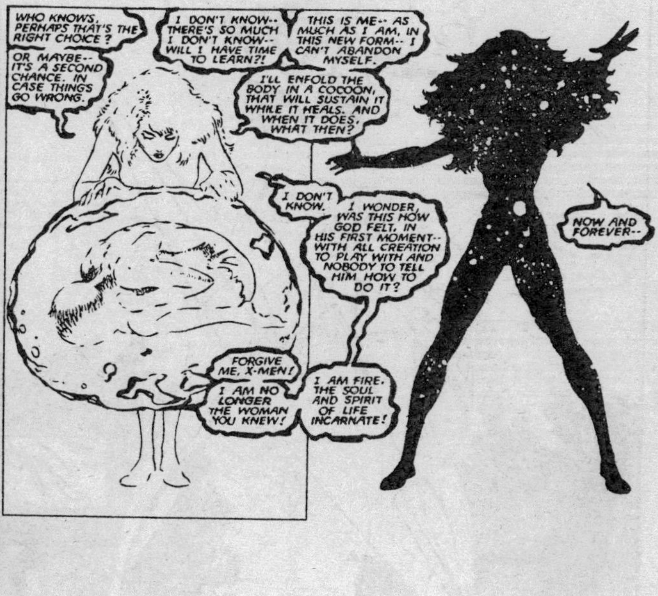
WHO KNOWS, PERHAPS THAT'S THE RIGHT CHOICE?
OR MAYBE-- IT'S A SECOND CHANCE. IN CASE THINGS GO WRONG.
I DON'T KNOW-- THERE'S SO MUCH I DON'T KNOW-- WILL I HAVE TIME TO LEARN?!
THIS IS ME-- AS MUCH AS I AM, IN THIS NEW FORM-- I CAN'T ABANDON MYSELF.
I'LL ENFOLD THE BODY IN A COCOON, THAT WILL SUSTAIN IT WHILE IT HEALS. AND WHEN IT DOES, WHAT THEN?
I DON'T KNOW.
I WONDER, WAS THIS HOW GOD FELT, IN HIS FIRST MOMENT-- WITH ALL CREATION TO PLAY WITH AND NOBODY TO TELL HIM HOW TO DO IT?
FORGIVE ME, X-MEN!
I AM NO LONGER THE WOMAN YOU KNEW!
I AM FIRE. THE SOUL AND SPIRIT OF LIFE INCARNATE!
NOW AND FOREVER--

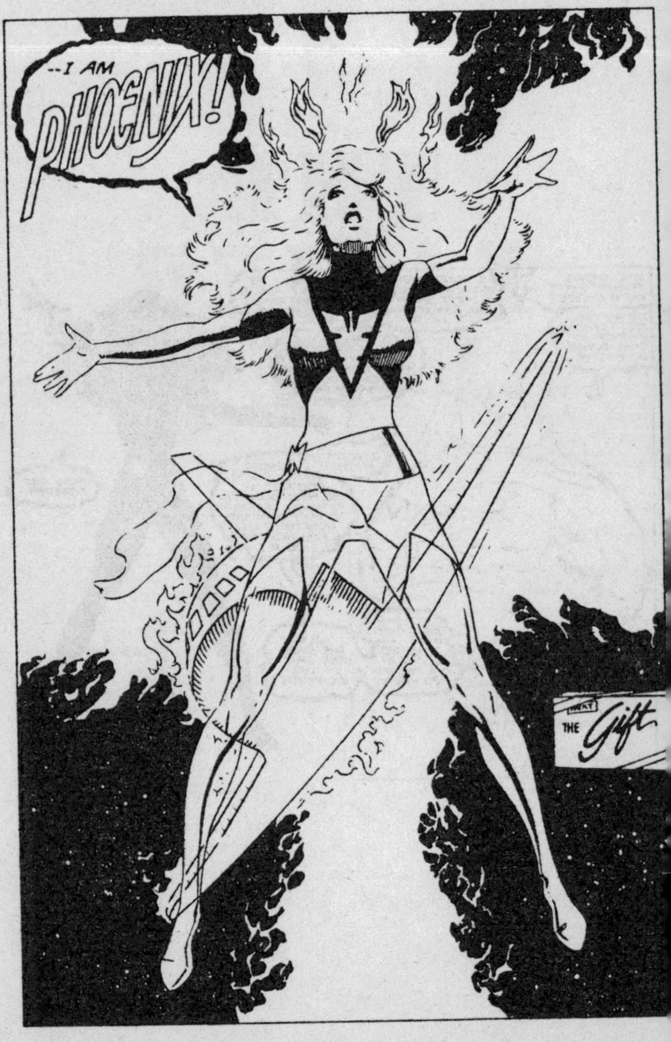

--I AM PHOENIX!
THE Gift

# THE
# XAVIER
# FILES

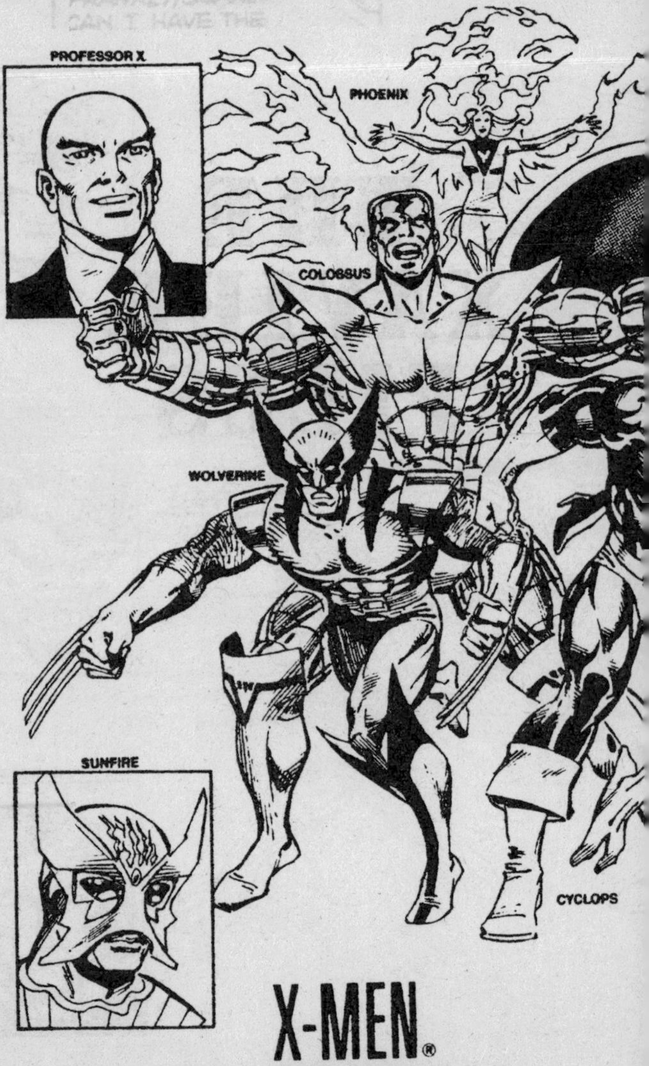
PROFESSOR X
PHOENIX
COLOSSUS
WOLVERINE
SUNFIRE
CYCLOPS

# X-MEN®
## THIRD LINE-UP

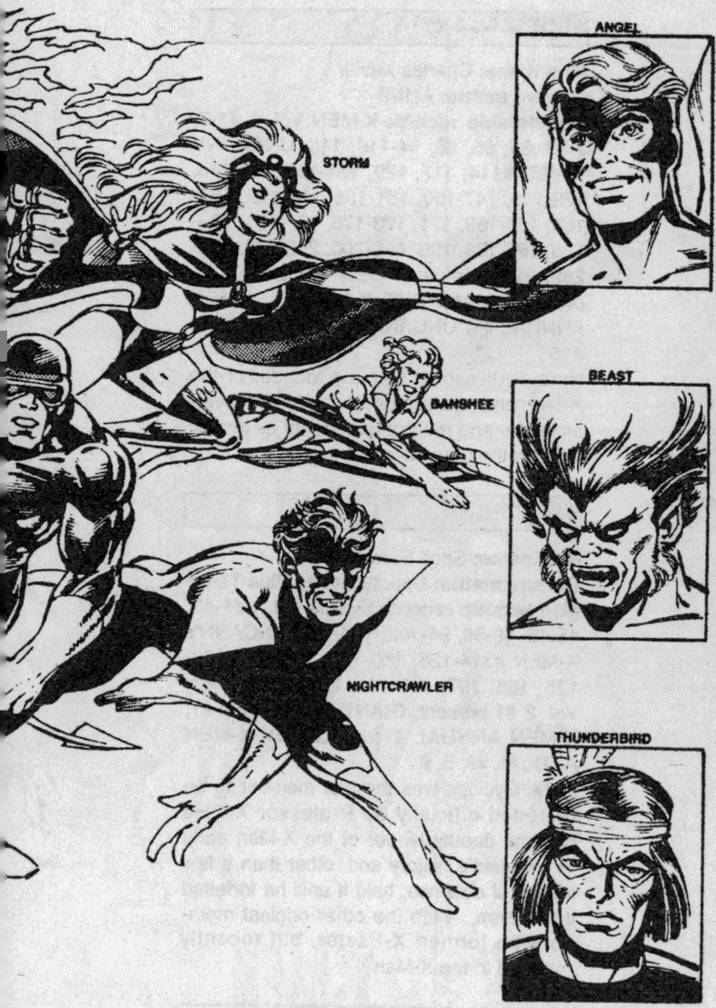
ANGEL
STORM
BEAST
BANSHEE
NIGHTCRAWLER
THUNDERBIRD

# X-MEN MEMBERSHIP ROSTER

## PROFESSOR X

**Real name:** Charles Xavier
**Current status:** Active
**Membership record:** X-MEN Vol. 1 #1-7, 9-33, 39, 65, 66, 94-110, 113; UNCANNY X-MEN #114, 117, 129, 131-133, 135-138, 139-145, 147-150, 151-158, 161-162, 164-165, 167-169, 171, 173-175, 177-181, 184-186, 188-193, 196, 199-200, 282-284, 286-289, 291-present; X-MEN Vol. 2 #1-5, 8-present; GIANT-SIZE X-MEN #1; X-MEN ANNUAL #1; UNCANNY X-MEN ANNUAL #16
**Note:** Professor X was the founder of the X-Men and has served as the team's overall leader and mentor for most of its history through the present

## CYCLOPS

**Real name:** Scott Summers
**Current status:** Deputy leader, Blue Team
**Membership record:** X-MEN Vol. 1 #1-43, 45-46, 49-66, 94-102, 104-113; UNCANNY X-MEN #114-138, 150-159, 161-168, 170-175, 185, 197, 199-201, 288-291; X-MEN Vol. 2 #1-present; GIANT-SIZE X-MEN #1; X-MEN ANNUAL #1; UNCANNY X-MEN ANNUAL #3, 5, 9
**Note:** Cyclops was the first member to be recruited officially by Professor X. He became deputy leader of the X-Men early in the team's history and, other than a few leaves of absence, held it until he forfeited it to Storm. With the other original members he formed X-Factor, but recently returned to the X-Men

## BEAST

**Real name:** Henry P. McCoy
**Current status:** Active, Blue Team
**Membership record:** X-MEN Vol. 1 #1-43,

46, 49-66; GIANT-SIZE X-MEN #1 (as a member), X-MEN Vol. 1 #111-113; UN-CANNY X-MEN #114, 134-137 (as a non-member ally); UNCANNY X-MEN #288; X-MEN Vol. 2 #1-3, 5-present

**Note:** The Beast was the fourth official recruit into the X-Men. He later served as a member of the Avengers, the Defenders, and the original X-Factor, but has since returned to the X-Men

## MARVEL GIRL

**Real name:** Jean Grey
**Current status:** Active, Gold Team
**Membership record:** X-MEN Vol. 1 #1-24, 27-43, 46, 49-66; UNCANNY X-MEN #281-present; X-MEN Vol. 2 #1-3, 8; GIANT-SIZE X-MEN #1; UNCANNY X-MEN ANN-UAL #16 (as member); X-MEN Vol. 1 #97-100 (as non-member ally)

**Note:** Though she was the fifth official recruit into the X-Men, Jean Grey had actu-ally been training under Xavier's tutelage since she was eleven. Although she quit the team, she became involved on an X-Men mission during which she was placed in suspended animation by the Phoenix Force, who then took on her identity and became known as Phoenix II. Years later, after the demise of Phoenix II, Jean was found and revived. She became a found-ing member of X-Factor. She has since rejoined the X-Men

## POLARIS

**Real name:** Lorna Dane
**Current status:** Inactive (active with X-Factor II)
**Membership record:** X-MEN Vol. 1 #49 (as Iceman's friend); GIANT-SIZE X-MEN #1, X-MEN Vol. 1 #94 (as a member), X-MEN Vol. 1 #50-51, 97 (as an antagonist), X-MEN Vol. 1 #52, 57-58, 60-61, UNCAN-NY X-MEN #125-129, 145-146, 158-159,

163, 173, 218, 249-250, 253 (as a non-member ally), UNCANNY X-MEN #219, 221-222, 239-241, 243 (as an antagonist possessed by Malice III), UNCANNY X-MEN #254-255. 257-258, 269, 280; UNCANNY X-MEN ANNUAL #15 (as member of Moira MacTaggart's X-Men)

**Note:** Polaris first met the X-Men when she was captured by Mesmero. She was recruited into the X-Men to aid in their battle against the alien Z'nox.

## HAVOK

**Real name:** Alexander "Alex" Summers
**Current status:** Inactive (active with X-Factor II)
**Membership record:** X-MEN Vol. 1 #65-66, 94, GIANT-SIZE X-MEN #1, UNCANNY X-MEN #218-219, 221-227, 229-235, 237-243, 245-251 (as a member); X-MEN Vol. 1 #54-61, 105, 119, UNCANNY X-MEN #125-129, 145-146, 158-159, 163, 168, 173, 175 (as a non-member ally); X-MEN Vol. 1 #97 (as an antagonist), UNCANNY X-MEN #270-272 (as a brainwashed antagonist); UNCANNY X-MEN ANNUAL #11-13 (as a member)

**Note:** Havok first became involved with the X-Men when he was captured by the Living Pharaoh and then by the Sentinels. Professor X recruited Havok into the X-Men to aid in their battle against the alien Z'nox.

## NIGHTCRAWLER

**Real name:** Kurt Wagner
**Current status:** Inactive (active with Excalibur)
**Membership record:** X-MEN Vol. 1 #94-UNCANNY X-MEN #170, 174-175, 177-181, 183, 186, 188-194, 196, 199-204, 206-213, 227; GIANT-SIZE X-MEN #1; UNCANNY X-MEN ANNUAL #3-10

**Note:** The German-born Nightcrawler was the first recruit into the new team of X-Men

organized by Professor X to rescue the
original X-Men from the Living Island
Krakoa.

## WOLVERINE

**Real name:** Logan
**Current status:** Active, Blue Team
**Membership record:** X-MEN Vol. 1 #94-
UNCANNY X-MEN #168; UNCANNY X-
MEN #172-176, 178-181, 183, 192-196,
199-203, 205, 207-216, 219-221, 223-230,
233-243, 245-246, 251-253, 257-258, 261,
268, 271-280; X-MEN Vol. 2 #1-present;
GIANT-SIZE X-MEN #1; UNCANNY X-
MEN ANNUAL #3-16; X-MEN ANNUAL
VOL. 2. #1
**Note:** The Canadian Wolverine resigned
from the team that would become known
as Alpha Flight when Professor X asked
him to join the new team of X-Men he organized for the Krakoa mission.

## BANSHEE

**Real name:** Sean Cassidy
**Current status:** Inactive
**Membership record:** X-MEN Vol. 1 #94-
UNCANNY X-MEN #129; X-MEN Vol. 2
#1-5; GIANT-SIZE X-MEN #1; UNCANNY
X-MEN ANNUAL #3
**Note:** After Professor X freed him from the
control of the subversive Factor Three, the
Irish-born Banshee became the X-Men's
ally against them. Xavier later recruited
him into the new team of X-Men assem-
bled for the Krakoa mission.

## STORM

**Real name:** Ororo Munroe
**Current status:** Active, Deputy leader,
Gold Team
**Membership record:** X-MEN Vol. 1 #94-
UNCANNY X-MEN #175, 177-181, 183,
185-194, 196-198, 201-203, 206, 208-210,

212-216, 219-227, 229-231, 233-239, 241-248, 253, 255, 257, 265-267, 270-278, 280-present; X-MEN Vol. 2 #1-3, 5, 8; GIANT-SIZE X-MEN #1; UNCANNY X-MEN ANNUAL #3-14

**Note:** Born in the United States, Storm grew up in Africa, where she was recruited by Professor Xavier for the new team of he had assembled for the Krakoa mission

## SUNFIRE

**Real name:** Shiro Yashida
**Current status:** Inactive
**Membership record:** X-MEN Vol. 1 #64 (as an antagonist); GIANT-SIZE X-MEN #1, X-MEN Vol. 1 #94 (as a member); UNCANNY X-MEN #118-120, 284-286 (as a non-member ally)
**Note:** The only Japanese X-Man, Sunfire was recruited by Professor X to help save the original X-Men from Krakoa.

## COLOSSUS

**Real name:** Piotr (Peter) Nikolaievich Rasputin
**Current status:** Active, Gold Team
**Membership record:** X-MEN Vol. 1 #94-UNCANNY X-MEN #175, 177-181, 183-184, 187-194, 196-197, 199-203, 206-213, 225-227, 229-241, 243-251 279-288, 290-present; X-MEN Vol. 2 #1, 3, 5 (as a member); UNCANNY X-MEN #259-260, 262-264 (as Peter Nicholas), UNCANNY X-MEN #277-278 (as an antagonist), GIANT-SIZE X-MEN #1; UNCANNY X-MEN ANNUAL #3-10, 12-13, 16
**Note:** A native of Russia, Colossus was recruited into the new X-Men team for the Krakoa mission.

## THUNDERBIRD I

**Real name:** John Proudstar
**Current status:** Inactive (deceased)

**Membership record:** GIANT-SIZE X-MEN #1, X-MEN Vol. 1 #94-95

**Note:** An Apache from Arizona, Thunderbird was recruited by Professor X to join the new team of X-Men assembled for the Krakoa mission. Thunderbird became the second X-Man to die in action when he was killed in the explosion of Count Nefaria's skycraft during his second recorded mission with the team.

## PHOENIX II

**Real name:** None, adopted persona of Jean Grey

**Current status:** Inactive (active as Phoenix III in Excalibur)

**Membership record:** X-MEN Vol. 1 #105-109 (as non-member ally), X-MEN Vol. 1 110-UNCANNY X-MEN #114, 117, 119, 122, 125-137 (as a member)

**Note:** The sentient cosmic entity known as the Phoenix Force created for itself a human body identical to that of Jean Grey (Marvel Girl), and took from her a portion of her consciousness. The X-Men believed that Phoenix was indeed Jean Grey and welcomed her back into their team. Mastermind used his powers to corrupt her psyche, triggering her change into the insane Dark Phoenix. Phoenix slew her human body rather than further menace the cosmos. The Phoenix Force later merged with Rachel Summers, the new Phoenix. The portion of Grey's consciousness within Phoenix infused itself into Madeline Pryor, and has since been restored to the psyche of Jean Grey herself.

# SENTINELS

The Sentinels are large semi-humanoid robots designed to locate and either capture or kill superhuman mutants. The creator of the Sentinels was the noted anthropologist Dr. Bolivar Trask. Although Bolivar Trask's principal field was anthropology, he also had considerable talents in biophysics, cybernetics, and robotics. Trask first became aware of mutants when he learned that his son Lawrence ("Larry") was a mutant with precognitive abilities. He then embarked on a private anthropological study of the rapidly increasing emergence of superhumanly powerful mutants in the world. He became convinced that these mutants were the first of a newly evolving race of humanity, and that they would use their powers to dominate the world and enslave humanity. Thus, three years before his death, Trask founded a small group of researchers, led by himself and his now adult son Larry, to compile evidence that superhumanly powerful mutants posed a threat to humanity. Then, using his considerable fortune, Bolivar Trask hired a large team of cyberneticists, roboticists, and engineers to construct the first Sentinels for him, following his basic ideas and designs. Bolivar Trask first publicly revealed the existence of the Sentinels in the course of a live televised debate between himself and the geneticist and anthropologist Professor Charles Xavier, the secret leader of the mutant X-Men on the subject of the alleged "mutant menace" to humanity (see *Professor X, X-Men*).

To date there have been five different models of the Sentinels. These are as follows.

*Mark I:* These are Bolivar Trask's original Sentinels. Because neither the Trasks nor any of their employees were as skilled as such roboticists as Doctor Doom and Machinesmith, they created machines whose workings they could neither entirely comprehend or control (see *Doctor Doom, Machinesmith*). The first Sentinels were programmed to protect humanity from mutants, but their logic led them to conclude that they could best do so by taking control of human society from the "imperfect" humans whom they considered to be their physical and intellectual inferiors. As a result, in the course of the aforementioned televised debate, one of the Sentinels attacked Bolivar Trask as he tried to give some of them orders, and they kidnapped him. Trask was brought to the fortress he had had

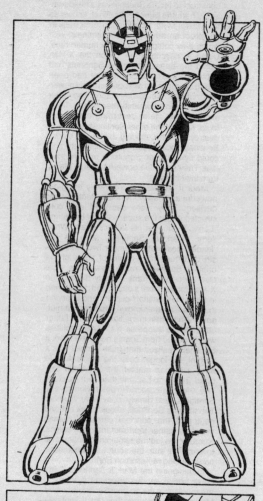

constructed for the Sentinels as a headquarters. There the principal Sentinel, known as the Master Mold, attempted to force Trask to construct an army of more Sentinels, with which they could conquer the human race. Using a "psycho-probe," upon the X-Man called the Beast, whom the Sentinels had captured, Trask realized that he had been wrong, and that not all superhumanly powerful mutants would inevitably use their abilities against humanity (see Beast). Trask sacrificed his life in destroying the Master Mold. Most of the other Sentinels were also destroyed in the ensuing explosion. Mark I Sentinels possessed great strength and could fly using jet propulsion units in their feet. They could fire powerful energy blasts from their chests.

*Mark II:* These are apparently the most powerful and nearly invincible Sentinels yet devised. They were designed and constructed under the supervision of Lawrence "Larry" Trask after his father's death. While some "Mark II" Sentinels, such as the "leader," designated Number Two, were constructed from the remains of some of the original Sentinels, many new ones were also built. Larry Trask wrongly blamed the X-Men for his father's death, and determined to have the Sentinels capture and imprison them and all other known superhuman mutants. When the medallion that his father gave him to suppress his mutant abilities was removed from Trask's neck, the Mark II Sentinels realized that Trask himself was a mutant. No longer believing themselves to have a human master, the Sentinels captured Trask and became their own masters. The X-Men succeeded in destroying several Sentinels, and finally convinced Number Two that the Sentinels should seek out and neutralize the principal cause of human mutation, rather than mutants themselves. Number Two led the remaining Sentinels off towards the sun, the source of most mutation-inducing radiation on Earth.

In designing the Mark II Sentinels, Larry Trask added various weapons systems to the robots that the original Sentinels lacked. Moreover, he designed the Mark II Sentinels' computer systems so that the Sentinels could instantaneously analyze whatever opposing force or combatant they encountered and rapidly ajust their mode of attack to cope with it. This factor made the Mark II Sentinels extremely difficult to defeat, although they were not indestructible, nor could they contain weapons systems capable of dealing with every possible danger to them.

Mark II Sentinels possessed vast strength and could fly via jet propulsion units in their feet. They could project strong steel tendrils, powerful force blasts, and jets of knockout gas or steam from their palms.

But while orbiting the sun, the Sentinels concluded that since they lacked the means to destroy the sun, the mutant problem had to be attacked by a different means. The solar heat and radiation somehow caused Number Two to become capable of killing humans in order to safeguard the Sentinels' overall goals. It also somehow developed the ability to create space warps. Number Two led the Sentinels back to Earth where, in the Great Australian Desert, they devised a means of triggering and controlling solar flares. The Sentinels' intent was to create a solar flare that would sterilize all of humanity, thus preventing mutants (and normal humans, as well) from being born. The Sentinels would then artificially create a new human race that would be incapable of mutation. The Avengers halted these plans, and all of the remaining Sentinels were deactivated or destroyed, and buried within a mound in the desert (see *Avengers*). In the course of all this, Larry Trask was killed.

*Mark III:* After the death of Larry Trask, ownership of the plans for the Sentinels fell under the control of the United States government. Dr. Steven Lang was placed in charge of a federal investigation of mutants that was intended to discover how mutations bestowing superhuman powers came about. Unknown to his employers, however, Lang had a fanatical, irrational distrust of superhuman mutants. He used his position to gain access to the Trask notes and designs, and then approached the Inner Circle of the Hellfire Club, which at that time was called the Council of the Chosen (see *Hellfire Club*). The Club provided Lang with the money he needed to construct new Sentinels and to create an orbiting space station headquarters, unaware that Lang's real intention was to destroy every superhumanly powered mutant he captured. Lang's Sentinels and space station were destroyed in a battle between the Sentinels and the X-Men. Although Lang was left a "mindless vegetable," he had imprinted his brain engrams in the computer-brain of his own 30-foot tall Master Mold, but it was destroyed in an encounter with the Hulk (see *Hulk*).

The Mark III Sentinels were inferior to the Trasks' since the notes Lang worked from

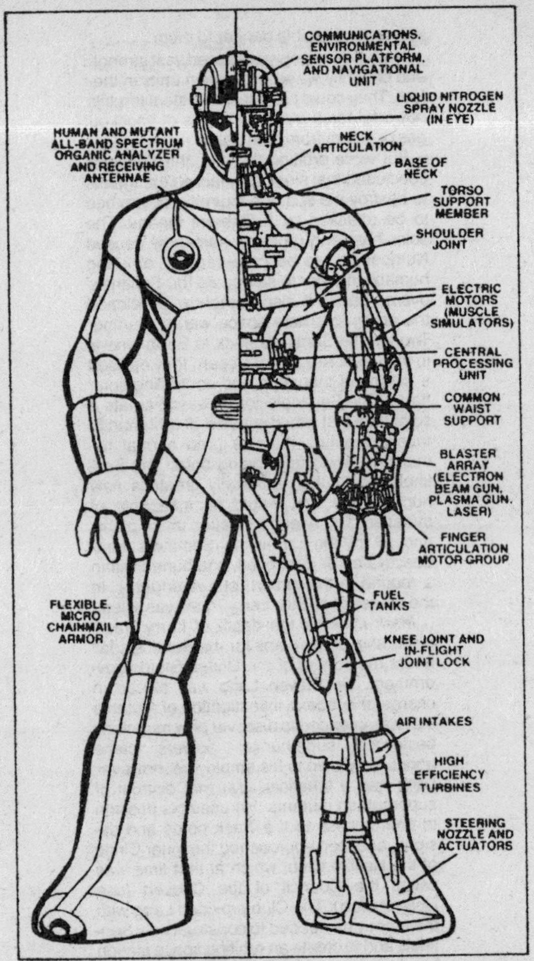
COMMUNICATIONS. ENVIRONMENTAL SENSOR PLATFORM. AND NAVIGATIONAL UNIT
LIQUID NITROGEN SPRAY NOZZLE (IN EYE)
HUMAN AND MUTANT ALL-BAND SPECTRUM ORGANIC ANALYZER AND RECEIVING ANTENNAE
NECK ARTICULATION
BASE OF NECK
TORSO SUPPORT MEMBER
SHOULDER JOINT
ELECTRIC MOTORS (MUSCLE SIMULATORS)
CENTRAL PROCESSING UNIT
COMMON WAIST SUPPORT
BLASTER ARRAY (ELECTRON BEAM GUN, PLASMA GUN, LASER)
FINGER ARTICULATION MOTOR GROUP
FUEL TANKS
FLEXIBLE. MICRO CHAINMAIL ARMOR
KNEE JOINT AND IN-FLIGHT JOINT LOCK
AIR INTAKES
HIGH EFFICIENCY TURBINES
STEERING NOZZLE AND ACTUATORS

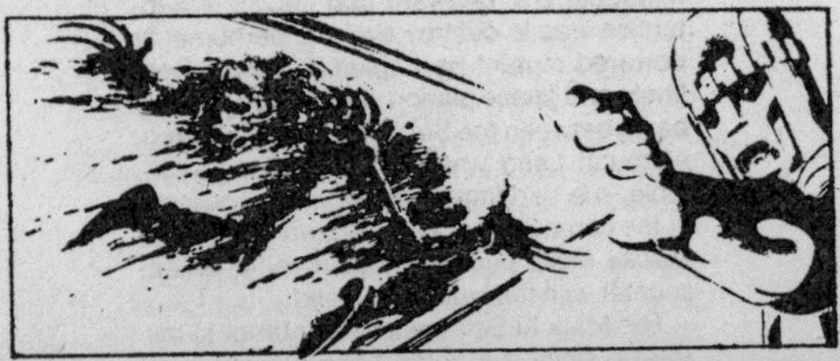

were incomplete, and because the secrecy surrounding his activities prevented him from hiring as many specialists as the Trasks could to help him build the Sentinels. Also, in order to ensure that these Sentinels could never rebel against him, Lang had to make them less intelligent than their predecessors. The Mark III Sentinels had great strength, could fly through jet propulsion systems in their feet, and could fire energy beams. Lang also built Sentinels in the forms of the original X-Men.

*Mark IV and V:* After the second Brotherhood of Evil Mutants' attempted assassination of Senator Edward Kelly (who was undertaking a public investigation of the possible menace posed by superhumanly powerful beings, especially mutants), the Office of the President inaugurated the secret and illegal "Project Wideawake," to investigate, and if need be capture, any superhumanly powerful mutant who the project directors believe may possibly pose a threat to "national security" (see *Freedom Force, Appendix: Kelly, Senator Robert*). The overall director of the project is special agent Henry Peter Gyrich of the National Security Council (see *Gyrich, Henry Peter*). As head of Project Wideawake, Gyrich is responsible only to the President. Senator Kelly is a special consultant to the Project, as is Sebastian Shaw, who, unknown to the government, is himself a mutant (see *Black King*). Shaw Industries, which Shaw owns and heads, has been licensed by the government under heavy secrecy to construct Sentinels for use by Project Wideawake, and by the Department of Defense. So far Shaw has produced two models of Sentinels, Mark IV and Mark V, both of which are regarded as prototypes for new model series now in development.

Without the knowledge of the government, Sebastian Shaw has used Sentinels to attack the X-Men in his role as the leader of the Hellfire Club. The government remains unaware of the Inner Circle's ambitions for world domination.

There are also two other known models of Sentinels, which were created in the future of an alternate Earth. In this alternate reality, the second Brotherhood of Evil Mutants succeeded in assassinating Senator Robert Kelly. As a result a presidential candidate was elected on an extreme anti-mutant platform, and his administration unleashed Sentinels, giving them a broad mandate to eliminate the mutant "menace" permanently. The

Sentinels did so by taking over the United States and the rest of North America, and killing or capturing virtually all superhuman beings, whether they were mutants or not. Captured mutants who were not killed were incarcerated in concentration camps called "mutant internment centers."

During this time a new model of Sentinel was created, the *Omega* series, which were especially designed for hunting and killing superhuman mutants. The specifications of the Omega series are unknown. Like other Sentinels, they have tremendous strength, are highly resistant to damage, and can fly using propulsion units in their feet. Omega Sentinels can fire energy blasts from their palms, and form non-metallic "catchwebs" from their fingers in order to imprison opponents. Omega Sentinels contain self-repairing systems. Like Mark II Sentinels they can analyze an opponent's abilities and adjust their weapons systems to deal with his or her powers.

During the Sentinels' reign in this alternate reality, "Project Nimrod" created the most advanced version of a Sentinel robot possible using that reality's technology. The product of Project Nimrod, the Sentinel called *Nimrod*, has traveled to our own reality, where it hunts superhuman mutants in the present (see *Nimrod*).

Information on the capabilities of the Mark IV and V Sentinels is as yet very sparse. Neither of the two new models appears to be as formidable as the Mark II series. Mark IV Sentinels are 20 feet tall and release steel tendrils from their hands. Model V Sentinels are 20 feet tall, can fly using jet propulsion units in their feet, release energy blasts and sleeping gas blasts from their hands, and project beams of intense cold from their eyes. They are equipped with sensors that can analyze both human and mutant opponents. Development work continues on Sentinels at Shaw Industries, and future models may be radically different from past Sentinels in many respects.

First appearance: (Mark I) X-MEN #14, (Mark II) X-MEN #57, (Mark III) X-MEN #98, (Mark IV) X-MEN #151, (Mark V) NEW MUTANTS #2, (Omega Sentinels) X-MEN #141 (first called by name in X-MEN #202), (Nimrod) X-MEN #191